USING
COMMON WORSHIP:
Marriage

The *Using Common Worship* series
Series editor: Mark Earey

Other titles include:
Funerals – R Anne Horton
Holy Communion – Mark Beach
Initiation Services – Gilly Myers

USING
COMMON WORSHIP:
Marriage

A Practical Guide to the New Services

Stephen Lake

 CHURCH HOUSE
PUBLISHING

For Carol, who makes solemn commitment such good fun

Church House Publishing
Church House
Great Smith Street
London SWIP 3NZ

ISBN   0 7151 2004 2

Published 2000 by Church House Publishing and *Praxis*

Second impression 2000

Copyright ©   *Stephen Lake 2000*

Telephone   020 7898 1557
Fax   020 7898 1449
Email   *copyright@c-of-e.org.uk*

Cover design by Silver Fish Creative Marketing

Typeset in 11pt Sabon and 11.5pt Gill Sans by Pioneer Associates (Graphic) Ltd, Perthshire

Printed by The Cromwell Press Ltd, Trowbridge, Wiltshire

Contents

What is *Praxis*?

Praxis was formed in 1990, sponsored by the Liturgical Commission of the Church of England, the Alcuin Club, and the Group for the Renewal of Worship (GROW). It exists to provide and support liturgical education in the Church of England.

Its aims are:

- to enrich the practice and understanding of worship in the Church of England;

- to serve congregations and clergy in their exploration of the call to worship;

- to provide a forum in which different worshipping traditions can meet and interact.

The name *Praxis* comes from the Greek word for action. It emphasizes our practical concerns and conveys our conviction that worship is a primary expression of the Christian faith.

Praxis runs an annual programme of day conferences and residential workshops around the country, organized either centrally or by *Praxis* regions (informal networks of diocesan liturgical committees).

You can find out more about *Praxis* from our web site: www.sarum.ac.uk/praxis/

For a copy of the *Praxis* programme and details of how to affiliate, contact the *Praxis* office:

Praxis
St Matthew's House
20 Great Peter Street
LONDON
SW1P 2BU
Tel: 020 7222 3704
Fax: 020 7233 0255
Email: praxis@stmw.globalnet.co.uk

Foreword

Those who produced the *Common Worship* services wanted to provide liturgical resources that encourage worshipping communities to take account of the pastoral needs of the congregation and the mission imperative of worship that engages with the surrounding culture.

The synodical process has, rightly, focused on the texts, the structures and the rubrics. But the services will only come to life and reach their potential as living encounters with God in the nitty-gritty of worship in parish churches, hospitals and prison chapels, school halls and other centres of worship. *Praxis* was set up by the Liturgical Commission in partnership with The Group for the Renewal of Worship (GROW) and the Alcuin Club to foster just such a practical approach to liturgy – working at grass roots level to support real churches who are seeking to make their regular worship better. *Praxis* has been running training events and courses to this end for ten years and it is a great step forward to see the combination of deeper understanding and better practice coming together in print.

The *Using Common Worship* series is a creative partnership between *Praxis* and Church House Publishing which will help all of us to make the most of *Common Worship*. Each volume bridges the gap between the bare texts and the experience of using those texts in worship. Full of practical advice, backed up with the underlying thinking from members of the Liturgical Commission, these books will be a valuable tool to put alongside the *Common Worship* volumes on the shelves of every worship leader in the Church of England.

✠ *David Sarum*
Chairman of the Liturgical Commission

Acknowledgements

The author would like to thank the people of St Aldhelm's Branksome for many years of shared ministry.

The author and publisher gratefully acknowledge permission to reproduce copyright material in this book. Every effort has been made to trace and contact copyright holders. If there are any inadvertent omissions we apologize to those concerned and undertake to include suitable acknowledgements in all future editions. Page numbers are indicated in parentheses.

The Anglican Church in Aotearoa, New Zealand and Polynesia: extracts taken/adapted from *A New Zealand Prayer Book – He Karikia Mihinare O Aotearoa* (p. 32, p. 55).

Cambridge University Press: extracts (and adapted extracts) from *The Book of Common Prayer*, the rights in which are vested in the Crown, are reproduced with permission of the Crown's patentee, Cambridge University Press.

The Faculty Office of the Archbishop of Canterbury: extracts from *Anglican Marriage in England and Wales: A Guide to the Law for Clergy*, 1992/1999 (Chapter 5).

The General Synod of the Anglican Church of Canada: extract adapted from *The Book of Alternative Services of the Anglican Church of Canada* copyright © 1985 by the General Synod of the Anglican Church of Canada. Used with permission (p. 67).

The International Commission on English in the Liturgy: English translations based on (or excerpted from) *The Roman Missal* © 1973 International Committee on English in the Liturgy (ICEL).

The Joint Liturgical Group of Great Britain: extract from *An Order of Marriage for Christians from Different Churches* © The Joint Liturgical Group of Great Britain, 1999. Used with permission (p. 94).

Jubilate Hymns: 'Lord our God, in our sin . . .', from *Church Family Worship*, Hodder & Stoughton, 1986. Words by Michael Perry © Mrs B Perry/Jubilate Hymns. Used by permission (p. 64).

Methodist Publishing House: extract from *The Methodist Worship Book* © 1999 Trustees for Methodist Church Purposes. Used by permission of Methodist Publishing House (p. 55).

Preface

My mother works part-time in a bridal shop. Each day she sees a succession of brides-to-be come in to enjoy a unique moment in their lives. The choosing of a stunning wedding gown to be worn 'on the most important day of your life' is a much looked-forward-to challenge. My mother enjoys sharing in the excitement of the moment and the drama of the final choice. These special times have familiar signs and common conversations. How long have you known each other? Let's see your ring! How many bridesmaids have you? So the drama unfolds. Mum always listens to find out if the wedding is to take place in church, the shop being just along the road from the parish in which I serve. Mum likes to think that I might see the bride-to-be in all her splendour in a few weeks' time. Between the two of us, we share in our different ways in the event that is the celebration of marriage.

The aim of this book is to share in that celebration by working through the new service of marriage that is part of the Church of England's new alternative liturgy, under the general title of *Common Worship*.

The way in which marriage is celebrated in society today is changing dramatically. The Church of England has recently revised its marriage service as part of a wholesale renewal of its liturgy as alternative to *The Book of Common Prayer*. Changing liturgy in a changing world places demands upon clergy and all those involved in enabling the public celebration of marriage. This book will study the new provision and offer practical advice for those whose task it is to lead couples through worship into a clearer and greater understanding of their commitment to each other.

This is a book for parish clergy and all who have responsibility in churches, and seeks to offer advice and examples of good practice.

It is not about any current debate about marriage, cohabitation, marriage breakdown or marriage following divorce.

It assumes no grounding in the new text and can be used by both new and experienced clergy new to the revised service.

Stephen Lake

Introduction
Andrew Burnham

The themes of the marriage ceremony are never far from the human heart and those who seek the Church's solemnization of their union are sometimes looking for a setting that, if not archaic or quaint, is at least hallowed by time. Yet the Church is never called upon to speak more plainly than when ministering to couples making their vows: they are to understand the permanent character of the commitment and the example of unselfish love which God in Christ has shown to the world.

The *Common Worship* Marriage Service is a fresh attempt to minister to the English people with beauty and vigour, not least by reflecting thoughtfully on the context in which present day marriages are set. In the first part of this essay some general topics are examined. *Common Worship* itself is defined, with liturgy as 'stages in a journey'. There is an investigation of an earlier distinction between betrothal and marriage ceremonies and how something of this distinction is built into the *Common Worship* order. This is followed by a brief discussion of ideas of 'separation, liminality and incorporation'. Next comes some thinking about how the Liturgy of the Word is sited: reading Scripture has not always been part of the Church of England Marriage Service. The first part of the essay ends with a consideration of questions of theological revolution and cultural change.

The second part of the essay looks more closely at what is in the *Common Worship* Marriage Service. This includes new provision for the calling of banns. There is a 'programme note' to be read privately by the congregation before the service. The Introduction consists of the Welcome, the Marriage Preface, the Declarations, the Collect, and the Readings. The Marriage itself consists of the exchange of Vows, the ring ceremonies, the 'putting asunder' declaration and the Blessing of the Marriage. The Registration of the Marriage, the Prayers and the Dismissal follow. There is comment on the provision for Holy Communion. The second part continues with mention of ecumenical provision, facilitated by *Common Worship*. The fact that marriage is not a service but 'a way of life made holy by God'[1] is recognized by the new Thanksgiving for Marriage, briefly discussed at this point, with its provision for couples to reaffirm marriage vows. Finally, there is a brief note about the new cultural context in which Christian marriage is solemnized.

Common Worship

Common Worship is the title of a whole set of liturgies and liturgical resources designed to equip the Church of England for worship in the early part of the twenty-first century. Despite rapid cultural change, the hope is that *Common Worship* (CW) will last long enough for *The Alternative Service Book 1980* (ASB) to take its place in history as the last of a series of experimental liturgies and the longest of a number of field trials. Certainly CW services, unlike the experimental liturgies that preceded them, are authorized until further notice. The last thirty-five years of the twentieth century saw, for the first time since the seventeenth century, a new set of authorized liturgies in the Church of England. Since *The Book of Common Prayer 1662* (BCP) has become literally irreplaceable, an authorized service, whenever there is an equivalent service in the BCP, must be an 'alternative service'.

Some of the 1928 material was repackaged in the 1960s as *Alternative Services: First Series*. Easily the most popular of these services has been *Series 1 Matrimony*. General Synod has extended its authorization until 2005, by which time it was hoped that it would be clear whether demand still existed for a traditional language marriage service. It would also be clear whether the authorization of Series 1 should be further extended or an antiqued version of CW Marriage be produced. One reason why Series 1 might not survive is that CW Marriage permits the BCP wording of the Declarations and Vows to be used: old jewels in a new setting.

Given the success of the ASB in the 1980s – it was successful to an extent which dismayed BCP enthusiasts – and the decision to extend its shelf-life from ten years to twenty years, it would be surprising if CW had not built on ASB and to some extent reproduced its material. Other than Order 1 for Holy Communion, the CW liturgy which is closest to its ASB forerunner is the Marriage Service.[2] After a section called 'The Welcome', the CW Marriage Service has a Preface, outlining Christian teaching about marriage. There are declarations in the service – for instance, 'N, will you take N to be your wife?' – and vows – 'I, N, take you, N, to be my husband.' There are the giving of rings and joining of right hands. The union is blessed, the registers are signed and prayers are said. The Holy Communion may be celebrated. All of this is as expected and much of the wording remains familiar.

Stages in a journey

Perhaps the most innovative aspect of *Common Worship* is that its services are presented as a series of stages; to put this in another way, what is implicit in almost all liturgy is here made explicit. The stages are not merely a matter of lay-out – though the structure has been made much clearer – nor simply a publishing device to catch the eye. The stages in the marriage liturgy – the calling of the banns, the declarations, the vows, the giving of rings, the nuptial blessing, the registration of the marriage and the intercessions – reflect the way human lives are ordered as a series of events. The stages of a well-designed liturgy reflect further that God in Christ enables Christians so to live that life is not just random succession ('one damn thing after another', as the saying on a 1915 postcard has it), but an ever-deepening participation in the love of God. That love itself is set out in a linear series, progressively, the mighty acts of creation, redemption and the hope of salvation.

Creation, redemption and the hope of salvation are expressed and encountered liturgically in the key ideas of 'gathering', 'transformation' and 'mission'. God creates and convenes – congregates, gathers – his people. Those who are gathered are transformed by word and sacrament and sent out in mission to the world. Nowhere is this clearer than in the Marriage Service, though for the Church of England marriage is not one of the two 'Sacraments of the Gospel'.[3] The couple arrive and are welcomed (*gather*), hear the Word and make their vows. Now *transformed* into husband and wife, one flesh, their lives together are a sign of God's love in a broken world.[4] In short, in their faithfulness to one another and to God, they are called to play their part in the Church's *mission*.

Betrothal and marriage

In one sense, then, the Marriage Service has three stages, with the Prayers and the Dismissal – corresponding to the living out of married life in the community – as the third. In another sense, as the 'Structure of the Service' shows, the service is in two parts.

The Welcome, the Preface, the Declarations and the Liturgy of the Word together form the first part of the service, the 'Introduction'. The second part of the service comprises the exchange of Vows, the Giving of Rings, the Proclamation of the Marriage, the Blessing of the couple, the Registration, the Prayers and the Dismissal. The rationale of the design is that the first part of the service, the Introduction, corresponds to the first part of the medieval rite, which often took place at the church door but which Cranmer moved 'into the Body of the Church'. The second part, the Marriage, corresponds to the second part of the medieval rite, during which the couple come to the altar for blessing and communion. The readings and the sermon symbolize the deepening and informing of the relationship of those who are preparing to move from the simple commitment of betrothal to the solemn commitment of Christian marriage.

Betrothal rites and ceremonies of solemnization, most clearly separate in the historical rites of the East, gradually came together in the West. By the tenth century betrothal and solemnization apparently occur on the same day and increasingly as two parts of the one liturgy. David Cressy, writing about the cultural practices of Tudor and Stuart England, mentions 'handfasting rituals, espousals ceremonies' and 'the sealing of matrimonial contracts'.[5] Contracts of spousals were of two main kinds. The first was *per verba de presenti* (literally 'through words concerning the present'), which amounted to saying 'I do'. The second was *per verba de futuro* (literally 'through words concerning the future') which was either a way of saying 'I will' or, more cautiously, was conditional upon acquiring property (much as modern couples might wait to get married until they can afford the deposit on a house). These spousals often utilized bits of the marriage liturgy. Contracted couples were not supposed to consummate the union in anticipation of its solemnization, though many did. The social pressure was such that most couples went on to marry but it was not until the Hardwicke Act of 1753 in England that customary marriage – what we would call 'common law marriage' – was suppressed in favour of the rites insisted upon by the state. (The Council of Trent had abolished clandestine marriages – marriage without a public marriage service – in Catholic Europe two hundred years earlier.)

It could be argued that our culture is increasingly separating betrothal and marriage and for them to become distinct once more in the marriage service is a small step towards recognizing this separation. This interpretation should not be pressed too far. Neither the Liturgical Commission nor the General Synod Pastoral Rites Revision Committee thought it appropriate to use the marriage service as a means of redesigning the Church's pastoral strategy, either in this respect or in respect of the marriage of a divorced person.

Separation, liminality and incorporation

The distinctness of betrothal and marriage, and the underlying notion of stages in a journey, may have become clearer in the CW Marriage Service but the thinking is not new. Kenneth Stevenson's suggestion that 'marriages should be phased'[6] is based on the three stages distinguished by Arnold Van Gennep:

'separation', 'liminality' and 'incorporation'.⁷ If betrothal is 'separation' and 'incorporation' is the marriage itself, 'liminality', says Stevenson, might correspond to some such ceremony as 'prayers at home, even around the bedchamber'.⁸

Stevenson would like to see a distinct service for each of the three stages. This would be the norm, he argues, and there would be shorter versions available. CW, as we have seen, recovers some of the distinctiveness of two of the stages – betrothal and marriage. It might be argued, in fact, that the Marriage is itself the 'liminality' rite. This is the point when the couple are truly on the threshold of their new life together. For Cranmer, 'incorporation' was surely the couple receiving communion together and thus, as one, becoming both a new part of the worshipping body and a new family within the life, civic and spiritual, of the parish. Though the Holy Communion may be celebrated as the context for the CW Marriage Service, the third stage, as we have seen, consists of the Prayers and the Dismissal, which bind the couple into the Church's witness to the reconciling love of God.

The Liturgy of the Word

Where, amidst the stages of the Marriage Service, should the Readings and Sermon be sited? The Marriage Service in the BCP entirely omitted the reading of Scripture for reasons that are no longer defensible. The sixteenth-century prayer books had envisaged the Holy Communion, with readings, being celebrated at the time of the marriage, or at any rate the same day. The 1662 BCP permits the couple instead to receive communion 'at the first opportunity after their marriage'. That reads as a note of realism; it seems that Cranmer's instruction was not being honoured and had fallen victim to the religious scruples of the Presbyterians. (Would the couple be in a state of spiritual readiness to receive communion?) Not only so, but the general public were already showing indifference to the invitation to receive communion.

Though BCP Matrimony has no readings, the service concludes with a homily 'if there be no Sermon declaring the duties of Man and Wife'. This homily alludes to New Testament teaching on marriage, from Ephesians 5, Colossians 3, and Chapter 3 of the first Epistle of 'Saint Peter, the Apostle of Christ, who was himself a married man'. Even in a modern translation, much of this sounds strange today. The wife as 'the weaker vessel' who must submit to the husband 'as unto the Lord' is not a modern perception. Nor would injunctions to practise 'chaste conversation coupled with fear' go down well in modern marriage ceremonies. One cannot imagine the modern woman eschewing 'the outward adorning of plaiting the hair, and of wearing of gold, or of putting on of apparel'.

1928 and Series 1 suggest a passage of Scripture as an alternative to Cranmer's concluding homily and provide a Collect, Epistle and Gospel for the Nuptial Eucharist which Cranmer had hoped would take place and which, because of the Anglo-Catholic movement, had lately begun to happen occasionally. Attempts to introduce readings into the marriage service have never been very successful. Readings and Sermon at the beginning (as in ASB) precede the Preface and thus turn that into a second homily, when, arguably, it has most impact as the first piece of extended prose. Readings and Sermon after the Marriage (as in Series 1 and also permitted in ASB) suggest that the marrying is to be done without first listening to what Scripture might have to say about marriage. The Readings and Sermon, instead of supplying the context and being integral to the solemnization, become a 'pep talk' afterwards; as arguably they are in Cranmer's rather pungent homily.

The CW Marriage Service re-examines the place of the Liturgy of the Word in the rite and sites it between the Declarations and the Vows. The Church thus offers Scripture and its exegesis to those who have declared their intention of marriage so that, as they make their vows, they make them in the light of the gospel and Christian teaching about marriage. As with all CW services there is a real sense of moving from stage to stage. One or two practical objections to this particular ordering, however, have some force. One objection is psychological: many clergy feel, as the couple themselves often do, that the service needs to move swiftly on, if only out of consideration for the feelings of the bride and bridegroom. A second objection is that, if they are to attend to Readings and Sermon, the couple will need to sit down, which again disrupts the flow. Accordingly the older practice of having the Readings and the Sermon – or just the Sermon – after the Marriage is permitted.

The solution which fits both the design of the CW Marriage Service and the dynamics of the traditional 30-minute wedding is to have one reading only, to place it straight after the Collect and allow the couple to remain standing during it. The Sermon (as Note 5 suggests) comes straight after the Blessing of the Marriage and before the Registration. This is about half-way through and if the place of register signing is nearby, the couple can move there and sit down to listen to the Sermon.

Theological revolution and cultural change

In the Readings and Sermon – the Word – the Church speaks plainly about marriage as an ordinance of God and a reflection of the life of the Trinity. No less important is the – in one sense or another – sacramental transformation of man and woman, through Declarations and Vows and Giving of Rings. Much remains as it has always been, and it is a characteristic of good liturgy that it is faithful to the tradition for which it is a vessel.

Of all Cranmer's services, the Solemnization of Matrimony is closest to the medieval rites of Sarum (Salisbury), Hereford and York. As with the 1549 Communion rite, however, the similarities to what has gone before belie the differences. The wording of the Declarations and Vows is close to that of the pre-Reformation sources, especially Sarum, which were also in the vernacular. Yet, as Kenneth Stevenson reminds us,[9] 'Gods holy ordeinaunce' replaces 'if holy chyrche it woll ordeyne' and the ring is not blessed. Cranmer thus follows Luther in dismantling the sacramental status of marriage but, as one expects with Cranmer, enough of the medieval superstructure remains to conceal theological revolution underneath liturgical evolution.

Something similar might be said about the change to the vows in 1928. To remove the wife's promise to obey her husband was a small enough change liturgically, but the social and theological implications were far-reaching. One of the few differences between 1928 and Series 1 is that Series 1 reverts to BCP practice to the extent of once more allowing the wife to obey her husband. (It might be argued, of course, that allowing the wife in effect to choose whether or not to say she will obey her husband has given substance to the popular saying, 'I am the boss of this house and I have my wife's permission to say so.') The liturgist would comment that for husband and wife to make the same vows to each other is an ancient practice, found in the Christian East and predating the medieval and Reformed emphasis on wifely obedience. Yet removing 'obey' (or making 'obey' optional) does not bring the Church to the same point, culturally or theologically, as when 'obey' was not part of the vow.

It is possible, of course, that, in an increasingly secular society, the Marriage Service will be used eventually only by couples one or both of whom take an active part in church life. Not only would this afford a new basis for discussion of issues such as 'obey'; it would become feasible for the law so to be changed that the Church of England, like some other churches, were able to insist on marriage preparation. Such a preparation, as with the catechumenate and initiation, might facilitate liturgical ceremonies that are preliminary to marriage, for instance a separate ceremony of betrothal. In the meantime, the first of the Notes following the CW Marriage Service ('Preparation') tells an increasingly secular culture that

---

1 Preparation

It is the custom and practice of the Church of England to offer preparation for marriage for couples who are soon to be married, as well as to be available for support and counselling in the years that follow.

———— **||** ————

The CW Marriage Service

The Banns

Provision for the Marriage Service begins with an innovation. The Supplementary Texts include Prayers at the Calling of the Banns. Thus what has sometimes appeared to be a perfunctory and tiresome legal formality may be recast as, in effect, the first stage of the marriage, a preliminary rite. Parish priests have sometimes felt embarrassed that the couple should visit church simply so that what might be a small and unrepresentative group of the general public may be formally asked if anyone knows 'any reason in law why they may not marry each other'. Now, by contrast, the couple may be invited to church where prayer will be offered for them. This is one of the two prayers suggested:

> Lord,
> the source of all true love,
> we pray for *these couples.*
> Grant to them
> joy of heart
> seriousness of mind
> and reverence of spirit,
> that as they enter into the oneness of marriage
> they may be strengthened and guided by you,
> through Jesus Christ our Lord.
> **Amen.**

'Oneness of marriage' has more than one meaning.

Pastoral Introduction

Most clergy will be glad that wedding congregations, which often contain people unfamiliar with church, as they wait for the service to begin may have the benefit of a 'programme note', as it were, for reading before the service, and a list of the items in the rite, headed 'the Structure of the Service'. (This Pastoral Introduction is a re-worked version of a feature of the New Zealand service book,[10] with some theological amplification.)

The Introduction: Welcome, Preface, and Liturgy of the Word

The first of the two sections, the Introduction, begins the service, not with the ASB's simple one-sentence Liturgy of the Word, but with the Welcome. The origin of human love in the mutual love of the persons of the Trinity is made clear in the Grace which, unusually for an Anglican service, becomes a greeting. The sentence from 1 John 4.16 ('God is love . . .') may still be used and, in common with the Holy Communion, a corporate prayer of preparation is provided, loosely based on the BCP collect for Quinquagesima.

Another matter of sequence has been the listing in the Preface of what the BCP described as the 'causes for which Matrimony was ordained'. The Preface itself is a thoroughly Reformed device in which exhortation and explanation take precedence over ceremony and symbol. (Yet, as Geoffrey Cuming has said,[11] some of the material is in Chaucer's *Parson's Tale*. Cranmer is summarizing medieval teaching on marriage and not designating new 'causes'.) In his *Censura* (1551) Martin Bucer had taken exception to the placing last of 'mutual society, help, and comfort'. His comment was heeded in the ASB revision and, following Genesis 2.18ff, the need for friendship and companionship is identified as the primary human need and therefore the first of the reasons why marriage is given by God. The placing of the ASB Preface almost verbatim in the Supplementary Texts of the CW Marriage Service will please some clergy and dismay others. Some will be pleased that the substance of their regular three-point sermon is not displayed as the main liturgical text. Others will find that the new Preface, though no less rich in ideas, has a less memorable structure and is therefore less versatile catechetically.

The differences between the ASB Preface and that in the Supplementary Texts of the CW Marriage Service are very small. 'The Scriptures' have become 'the Bible'. '[Marriage] is given, that they may have children and be blessed in caring for them and bringing them up' has been replaced by '[Marriage] is given as the foundation of family life in which children may be born and nurtured'. 'They will (each) give and receive a ring' replaces 'they will give and receive a ring'. The greatest infelicity in what is otherwise a good piece of writing is unchanged. Marriage is still to be undertaken 'reverently, responsibly, and after serious thought'.

The new Preface (as printed in the main text of the service) has no 'holy mystery' and no 'one flesh'. The notion that the couple 'may find strength, companionship and comfort' is felicitous, as is the notion that 'marriage is a sign of unity and loyalty . . . [which] enriches society and strengthens community'. We still have 'reverently and responsibly' but 'in the sight of Almighty God' replaces 'serious thought', which is certainly a move from transience to transcendence. God becomes active as 'we pray with them that the Holy Spirit will guide and strengthen them' replaces 'strengthened and guided by God'.

The Declarations

What has been dubbed 'the most expensive Revision Committee in the life of the General Synod' took place in the autumn of 1999 when the Pastoral Rites Revision Committee was reconvened following a motion of re-committal at the July sessions of the General Synod. Its task was to consider the letter 's' at the end of the phrase 'forsaking all others'. 'Other' or 'others'?

There was always a suspicion that this was, at root, another issue about what is current English usage, though the Bishop of Norwich had argued earlier at a meeting of the Revision Committee that 'other' (BCP) indicated appropriately a forsaking of all other distractions and priorities, including 'other' sexual partners. Surely the Latin text in the Sarum Manual would provide the answer? This point was pursued in the General Synod by a supporter of the Bishop. 'The most expensive Revision Committee' was convened and consulted Paul Bradshaw, Professor of Liturgy at the University of Notre Dame, who reported that the Latin *omnes alios/alias* (literally, 'all other masculine/feminine ones') clearly meant other men and women and not other things. If the Revision Committee had chosen 'other', it could have done so only on the grounds of retaining a well-wrought English phrase. Some would say that in continuing to recommend 'others', it underestimated the power of the Church's services to affect language use in the wider culture and the subtlety of meaning in the older version. Nonetheless, 'forsaking all others' retains the resonance of the medieval phrase and is a succinct way of describing the spouse's single-minded attention to the future marriage.

The CW Marriage Service has a much surer sense than its predecessors of the importance of helping members of wedding congregations to understand and participate in the service. CW comes up with a new question, directly addressed to the congregation:

Will you, the families and friends of N and N,
support and uphold them in their marriage
now and in the years to come?
All **We will.**

This is somewhat parallel to the question in the Ordinal when the people are asked whether they will uphold the newly-ordained in their ministry.

Collect and Readings

The Collect also is new. The 1928 collect, which became the collect in ASB Marriage, has as a main idea the teaching that 'love is the fulfilling of the law'. Those who know their Bible well will understand this idea and be edified by it. Others will be puzzled, perhaps, by the apparent linking of conjugal love with obeying the law of the land. The new collect asks God who has 'blessed creation with abundant life' to pour out his blessings on the couple. The purpose of this outpouring is to be 'mutual love and companionship', 'holiness and commitment to each other', though the reference to 'abundant life' implies not only the life in abundance of John 10.10 but, where appropriate, the fruitfulness of Genesis 1.28.

For the 'Liturgy of the Word' (a heading used in the CW Marriage Service, incidentally, only when Holy Communion is celebrated), the Supplementary Texts offer 22 readings (double the provision of ASB) and four psalms (Psalm 127 as well as the three in ASB). The following psalms and readings, specified in the ASB, continue unmodified.[12] (Three that have been slightly modified are mentioned below.)

Psalm 67
Psalm 121
Psalm 128

Romans 12.1, 2, 9-13	('... present your bodies as a living sacrifice')
1 Corinthians 13, 1-13	('If I speak in the tongues ...')
Ephesians 3.14-21	('I bow my knees before the Father ...')
Ephesians 5.21-33	('Wives, be subject to your husbands ...')
Colossians 3.12-17	('Bear with one another ...')
1 John 4.7-12	('Beloved, let us love one another ...')
John 2.1-11	(The wedding in Cana of Galilee)

The readings that are additional to those in ASB are these:

Song of Solomon 2.10-13; 8.6-7	('My beloved speaks ...')
Tobit 8.4-8	(Tobias and Sarah pray)
Jeremiah 31.31-34	('I will make a new covenant ...')
Romans 7.1-2, 9-18	('A married woman is bound by the law ...')
Romans 8.31-35, 37-39	('If God is for us, who is against us? ...')
Romans 15.1-3, 5-7,13	('May the God of steadfastness and encouragement grant you to live in harmony with one another ...')
Ephesians 4.1-6	('bearing with one another in love ...')
Philippians 4.4-9	('Rejoice in the Lord always ...')

I John 3.18-24	('we should believe in the name of his Son . . . and love one another . . .')
Matthew 5.1-10	(The Beatitudes)
John 15.1-8	('I am the true vine . . .')
John 15.9-17	('abide in my love . . .')

There are additionally, as compared with the ASB, one or two changes of length of reading. What had been Genesis 1.26-28, 31a loses verse 31a. Matthew 7.21, 24-27 is extended to include verses 28-29. Mark 10.6-9 gains verses 13-16.

The Marriage: The Vows

Since the Vows are intentionally separated from the Declarations by Reading(s) and Sermon, a new link is scripted, an invitation to join hands and make vows. Already in the ASB there were signs of embarrassment with the concept of the bride's father 'giving her away'. The ceremony was optional and 'if the bride is not given away by her father, this might be done by another member of her family, or by a friend representing the family'.[13] Yet the rubric in the main text remained, 'The priest may receive the bride from the hands of her father.'[14]

CW does away with the reference in the main text, though a 'Giving Away' ceremony is provided in Note 6. Also the bride's mother is explicitly mentioned as one who may do the 'giving away'. But replacing the 'giveth' of the BCP question, the minister may ask 'Who *brings* this woman to be married to this man?'

Note 6 also provides a different form of challenge as an alternative to the traditional 'giving away' ceremony. The minister asks:

N and N have declared their intention towards each other.
As their parents,
will you now entrust
your son and daughter to one another
as they come to be married?

Both sets of parents respond:

We will.

This question has been phrased with some ingenuity. The text (though not the rubric) would work with only one parent of each set present.

The Vows have a new sentence in place of the final phrase. In place of 'and this is my solemn vow' bridegroom and bride say to each other 'In the presence of God I make this vow.' The Vows in the main text are symmetrical: bridegroom and bride make essentially the same vow. Alternative Vows in the Supplementary Texts (Form 1), provide modern language complementary vows, allowing brides who wish to obey their husbands to do so and (Form 2) traditional language versions of both the symmetrical and the complementary type of vow.

The Rings

The ring ceremony in CW is unchanged from ASB, except in two small respects. First, there is an alternative 'Prayer at the Giving of the Rings' in the Supplementary Texts, based on Song of Solomon 8 and 1 Corinthians 13:

Heavenly Father, source of everlasting love,
revealed to us in Jesus Christ
     and poured into our hearts through your Holy Spirit;
that love which many waters cannot quench,
     neither the floods drown;
that love which is patient and kind, enduring all things without
     end;
by your blessing, let these rings be to N and N
symbols to remind them of the covenant made this day
through your grace in the love of your Son
and in the power of your Spirit.
Amen.

Second, the version of the bride's words when she is not giving a ring to her husband, though identical to the ASB version, is now printed after the version when she gives a ring. A social anthropologist might infer, and probably correctly, that the use of two rings instead of one has grown in popularity since 1980.

Putting asunder

Another new feature in CW Marriage is the replacement of the ASB's 'That which God has joined together, let not man divide.' This phrase had been a victory for biblical scholarship over common sense and – for some congregations – in offensively exclusive language. A comparison between BCP and CW at this point reveals much about the approach of CW to the tradition, as compared with the brave iconoclasm of the ASB service:

BCP   Those whom God hath joined together let no man put asunder.

CW   Those whom God has joined together let no one put asunder.

'Put asunder' is one of those pieces of text that, at first sight, is no longer current English usage yet, like biblical phrases such as 'nothing new under the sun', has gained enough momentum to continue in use well after people forget the original context.

The Proclamation

In BCP the blessing of the couple follows the proclamation of the marriage (which itself follows the joining of hands). ASB and CW have the proclamation of the marriage before the 'let no one put asunder' phrase. The intention is to make it clear that, in the West at least, the couple are the ministers of marriage. It is they who 'tie the knot', whether or not the priest seems, by wrapping a stole around their hands, to be the one who is doing so. What the priest is doing, of course, is highlighting the solemnity of the vows and the sacredness of the marriage bond. Interestingly, the joining of hands and proclamation, which feel like the climax of the service and seem to be a sacramental, or quasi-sacramental, moment, are not found in the Sarum rite. Cranmer borrowed them from Hermann who borrowed them from Luther (who, admittedly, was using medieval German material).

The Nuptial Blessing

In a marriage service the Church highlights the solemnity of Christian marriage, provides a public context and, where this is possible, acts as registrar on behalf of the state. In addition it prayerfully provides a nuptial blessing. Nuptial blessings in the medieval West[15] include a history of blessing of the bride alone, as a fount of new life, but in the pre-Reformation English rites that Cranmer used, nuptial blessings were blessings of the couple. Since the heaping up of blessings was an English characteristic, it is no surprise that, in addition to Holy Communion (in itself a nuptial blessing), Cranmer has at least two other blessings. One is the 'God the Father, God the Son, God the Holy Ghost' blessing which follows the proclamation of the marriage. The other is the blessing at the end of the service. The second BCP blessing (immediately before the homily) mentions the precedent of the sanctifying and joining together of Adam and Eve and is a blessing of the couple only, that they too may be sanctified and blessed.

The ASB carefully wove together both the BCP blessings (they were both from the Sarum Manual) and the composite blessing is retained by CW. The final blessing in ASB, a blessing of 'the couple and the congregation', is arguably not a 'nuptial blessing' but the requisite liturgical ending which Cranmer had omitted (perhaps because he had intended a celebration of Holy Communion to follow on). This becomes clearer in CW where it becomes merely implicit that the couple are included in the blessing in the dismissal rite. CW follows ASB in using here the Holy Trinity blessing first found in the propers for ASB Rite A Eucharist. The learned will recall that the Nuptial Mass in the Sarum rite was a Mass of the Holy Trinity. Even those who do not know this will notice Trinitarian imagery in the Marriage Service: as has already been noticed, the Trinitarian context was established in the Grace at the beginning of the service.

The ASB nuptial blessing, as well as combining the two BCP nuptial blessings into one prayer, continued with an optional set of acclamations based on the seven blessings of bride and groom in Jewish marriage rites.

CW adapts this slightly (as one of several alternative forms – changes are underlined):

> Blessed are you, heavenly Father.
> *All* **You give joy to bridegroom and bride.**
> Blessed are you, Lord Jesus Christ.
> *All* **You bring life to the world** [*formerly* have brought life to mankind[16]]
> Blessed are you, Holy Spirit of God.
> *All* **You bind us together in love.** [*formerly* bring us together . . .]
> Blessed are you, Father, Son and Holy Spirit, now and for ever.
> > [now and for ever *has been added in place of the response* One God, to be praised for ever.]
> *All* **Amen.**

Since these acclamations require congregational participation and since experience teaches that some wedding congregations scarcely participate even in 'Praise, my soul, the King of heaven' and the Lord's Prayer, CW has moved the acclamations into the Supplementary Texts, where they form one of five sets of material and may be added to any of the other four sets.

The CW nuptial blessing is redesigned so that, instead of acclamations or other forms following the composite prayer of blessing ('God the Father, God the Son, God the Holy Spirit'), the optional forms precede the composite prayer. In the main text, the prayer preceding the composite prayer was reshaped by the Pastoral Rites Revision Committee into a *berakah* prayer: 'Blessed are you, O Lord our God . . .'.

Berakot – blessing God's name for this and for that – are one of the characteristic ways of praying in Jewish spirituality. The New Testament contains one or two outstanding instances of this form of prayer: the Song of Zechariah in praise of the Incarnation (Luke 1.68-79), and a *berakah* in praise of the Resurrection (1 Peter 1.3-9).

The new *berakah* prayer has in it two of the age-old images of nuptial blessing, the 'seal' of Song of Solomon 8.7 and the 'crown' of Isaiah 61.10. The 'mantle' (or 'canopy') found in Jewish marriage rites, and in many Christian ones too, was edited out of the prayer by the Revision Committee. The earlier version was:

> Let their love for each other be a seal upon their hearts,
> a mantle about their shoulders,
> and a crown upon their foreheads.

This has become:

> Let their love for each other be a seal upon their hearts,
> and a crown upon their heads.

While regretting the loss of 'mantle', we are grateful that the crown is on the head rather than the forehead.

The Registration, Prayers and Dismissal

The Registration of the Marriage follows the nuptial blessing, though Note 10 allows it to occur slightly earlier, after the Proclamation, or rather later, at the end of the service. The Prayers in the main text are new and in litany form. A rubric introduces the litany and assists those who select prayers from the Supplementary Texts or elsewhere.

> *The prayers usually include these concerns and may follow this sequence:*
>
> *Thanksgiving*
>
> *Spiritual growth*
>
> *Faithfulness, joy, love, forgiveness and healing*
>
> *Children, other family members and friends*

The litany itself has five sections: the second and third concerns in the rubric are woven into three of the five.

The catena of alternative prayers in the Supplementary Texts includes many that are also in litany form. The three prayers from the ASB main text are retained, as are one or two of the ASB's 'Additional Prayers', but there is much in the

Supplementary Texts that is new. As well as the Liturgical Commission's own work (e.g. prayer 1), there is 'A prayer for all people' (?) and several other prayers (e.g. 14, 15, 16, 18, 24, 25, 26) adapted from *A Prayer Book for Australia.*[17] There is material from New Zealand (e.g. 6). One prayer (4) is based on the *Book of Common Order*[18] and two (11 and 17) are adapted from the Joint Liturgical Group material.[19]

Most of the new material is on familiar themes – discipleship, the home, faithfulness – but the Australian prayer 15, 'For the healing of memory', strikes a new note:

> Loving God,
> you are merciful and forgiving.
> Grant that those who are suffering the hurts of the past
>   may experience your generous love.
> Heal their memories, comfort them,
> and send them all from here
> renewed and hopeful
> in Jesus Christ our Lord.
> *All* **Amen.**

Australia also provides resources for praying for an existing family (prayer 25):

> God of all grace and goodness,
> we thank you for this new family,
> and for everything parents and children have to share;
> by your Spirit of peace draw them together
> and help them to be true friends to one another.
> Let your love surround them
> and your care protect them,
> through Jesus Christ our Lord.
> *All* **Amen.**

As in ASB, the Prayers conclude with the Lord's Prayer. The Dismissal, as has already been mentioned, is the Holy Trinity blessing.

Related Issues

Holy Communion

The treatment of Holy Communion at the CW Marriage Service is gently innovative. The BCP tradition was for Holy Communion to follow the marriage service. ASB had two orders. In the first, the marriage ceremony took place between the Liturgy of the Word and the Liturgy of the Eucharist. In the second, the marriage ceremony preceded the Eucharist, as in BCP. CW follows the first of these patterns but, as compared with the service without Communion, recasts the Introduction so that Prayers of Penitence precede the Preface (of the Marriage Service). Readings and Sermon are taken out of the Introduction and called the Liturgy of the Word. A Gospel Reading becomes mandatory. The section called The Marriage is treated similarly: all is as in the simple order until the Registration of the Marriage. The Prayers and the Dismissal are taken out of the Marriage and become two new sections, one before and one after the Liturgy of the Sacrament. Propers include Prayers of Penitence and Gospel Acclamation, Introduction to the Peace, a prayer for the Preparation of the Table and the Gifts, short and long Prefaces in the Eucharistic Prayer and the Prayer after Communion. For the Dismissal, the Aaronic Blessing ('The Lord bless you and keep you . . .'), a feature of 1928 and Series 1, is given.

Ecumenical provision

Note 13 specifies how a minister of another Christian Church may take part in the Solemnization of Matrimony. The 'permissions and procedures set out in the Canon B 43 are to be followed'.

More radically (though there is no space to give details here) an Order is available for a couple who come from different communions. Devised by the (ecumenical) Joint Liturgical Group, 'An Order for the Marriage of Christians from Different Churches'[19] has the legal status of being the service of the Church of England when the bishop authorizes its use. It cannot be used, of course, for the marriage of two Anglicans.

Thanksgiving for Marriage

The Church's pastoral strategy is much enriched by a fuller provision of official liturgical material. The *Rites on the Way* resources (available as GS Misc 530) will help those preparing for the Initiation Services and there is provision for before and after funerals. Amongst the Pastoral Services that are commended rather than authorized[20] is Thanksgiving for Marriage. This service will be useful for reaffirming vows, whether to celebrate an anniversary or, indeed, after a time of separation or difficulty. Some may use the service for the dedication of a civil marriage, though this is not among the uses specified and the existing dedication service remains extant. The shape and much of the wording of Thanksgiving for Marriage is similar to the CW Marriage Service: Welcome, Prayer of Preparation (the ASB marriage collect), Preface, Readings and Sermon, Renewal of Vows, the Giving of Rings, Prayers, Dismissal. There is no equivalent of the Declarations, of course, and the Blessing is a simple blessing of couple and congregation.

An Outline Order is provided. Just as Free Churches have been embracing increasingly the richness of set liturgical texts, the Church of England, first in *Patterns for Worship* and A Service of the Word, has been exploring the freedom of the Outline Order. The Marriage Service, unusually amongst CW services, has no Outline Order: the law requires that the form of the Marriage Service is prescribed in detail.

Cultural context

For the first time ever the Church of England has produced a marriage service in what might be described as a highly competitive market. Only a few years ago a church wedding was the wedding of choice: those who were married elsewhere were choosing a ceremony based on a different religious perspective or a somewhat drab ceremony without God. Nowadays exciting alternatives to Gothic doorways and nave aisles are on offer. Even 'altar' may refer to the registrar's table on a Caribbean beach rather than the altar of God to which a couple go on the first journey of their married life. How the new Marriage Service fares in the market place is impossible to guess but couples who look to it for the solemnization of a truly religious commitment to each other will surely not be disappointed.

Notes

1 The Preface to the *Common Worship* Marriage Service.
2 A discussion of the ASB Marriage Service, its historical context and its innovations, is given in R. C. D. Jasper and Paul F. Bradshaw, *A Companion to the Alternative Service Book*, London, SPCK, 1986, pp. 373ff.
3 Article XXV.
4 Cf CW Marriage Service, Additional Prayers and Collects, Prayer 13, 'For marriage as a sign to the world'.
5 David Cressy, *Birth, Marriage and Death*, OUP, 1997, p. 233.
6 Kenneth Stevenson, *To Join Together: The Rite of Marriage*, New York, Pueblo Publishing, 1987, p. 190.
7 Arnold Van Gennep, *Les Rites de Passage*, Paris, 1909. Van Gennep's terms for 'separation', 'liminality' and 'incorporation' are *préliminaires (separation), liminaires (marge) et postliminaires (agrégation)*.
8 Kenneth Stevenson, *To Join Together: The Rite of Marriage*, New York, Pueblo Publishing, 1987, p. 192.
9 Kenneth Stevenson, *Nuptial Blessing*, London, 1982, pp. 135f.
10 *A New Zealand Prayer Book – He Karikia Mihinare O Aotearoa*, Auckland, 1989.
11 Geoffrey Cuming, *A History of Anglican Liturgy*, London, Macmillan, 1982, p. 63.
12 Scripture quotations are from the New Revised Standard Version.
13 See ASB, p. 285, note 5.
14 See ASB, pp. 290f.
15 See Kenneth Stevenson, *Nuptial Blessing*, pp. 35ff.
16 'The world' was suggested by *Making Women Visible*, London, 1988.
17 *A Prayer Book for Australia*, Alexandria, NSW, 1995.
18 *Book of Common Order*, Edinburgh, 1994.
19 Published separately as *An Order for the Marriage of Christians from Different Churches*, Canterbury Press Norwich, 1999.
20 Thanksgiving for Marriage is 'commended' rather than 'authorized' because it is not technically an 'alternative service', that is, there is no service in the BCP to which it is an alternative.

1 Preparation for the Marriage Service

1 Preparation
It is the custom and practice of the Church of England to offer preparation for marriage for couples who are soon to be married, as well as to be available for counselling and support in the years that follow.

(From the Notes to the Marriage Service)

A priest once said to me that he never gave marriage preparation. Somewhat taken aback, I questioned what he meant by this statement. His position was that he was not qualified to prepare couples for married life, but that he was qualified to prepare couples for the Marriage Service that would begin their married life together. Most churches would wish their clergy to offer some form of marriage preparation, possibly including the ministry of lay people, but clergy must provide good preparation for the celebration of the marriage moment itself. The new service presumes that this preparation will take place and that it will be given a high priority. In many ways, the key to good marriage preparation is to be found in the preparation for the liturgical celebration.

Such preparation for the great day may include:

- a warm welcome when an enquiry is made;

- clear information on administrative arrangements and legal requirements;

- personal contact;

- teaching about the chosen service, music, readings;

- discussion and teaching about the meaning and commitment of marriage;

- attentive rehearsal.

These elements are essential if couples are to become engaged (excuse the pun) with the Christian understanding of what they are asking the Church to provide for them.

A warm welcome

Most marriage enquiries come over the telephone. Sometimes a caller at the vicarage door may ask, 'Will you marry me?' This can cause temporary difficulties if the minister's married partner is elsewhere in the house but however the enquiry comes, a warm welcome is essential. As a church, we welcome marriage, we are pleased it takes place, and surely even more pleased if the request is for a service in church. The bearer of this news is usually thrilled to be telling the minister, who in this brief moment represents the response of the Church universal and, dare I say, Almighty God, to the engaged couple. A hurried reply about dates, fees and parish boundaries tends not to inspire. A warm welcome should include an expression of pleasure at the news and an assurance that sound advice will be given. The principle also applies when parish secretaries and others are the first to answer an enquiry, especially over the telephone. Often a personal appointment is then made or a general conversation continues about suggested dates to be pencilled in for the great day and other basic information is exchanged. Saying no to ineligible couples is best done face to face. Although costly in time, it is the correct pastoral engagement and should still include sound advice about the best path for the couple.

Clear information

Whether face to face or on paper there is a need for clear information about administrative arrangements and legal requirements. Best practice suggests that parishes provide a leaflet that can be sent or given to couples, outlining the parish policy on marriage, the general process and timetable from enquiry to marriage service, answers to commonly asked questions and practical information such as telephone numbers and service times. Other resources are also available such as:

Marriage, a colourful leaflet produced by The National Society/CHP;

Your Wedding by Mary Thompson, published by Ecclesiastical Insurance;

Your Wedding in the Church of England, published by Kevin Mayhew.

No doubt other publications will become available to accompany the new *Common Worship* service in due course.

This is often also the moment when legal requirements are discussed and this area requires clarity and sensitivity. Couples should be helped to understand the importance of the law in relation to a marriage and the subsequent implications in each individual case. Here is the point at which ineligible couples can feel rejected and so this needs careful management. It should always be the case that ineligible couples are guided to their next course of action and valued despite their ineligibility.

Clarity and sensitivity are also needed when the time comes to discuss fees, for even though the marriage service may be the cheapest part of the day, the concept of fees is new to some. We need to keep up with the cost of wedding days so as to be able to describe the context and then to be very clear what fees are for, e.g.:

- the use of a competent musician such as the organist;

- the use of a building that requires upkeep;

- the work of the clergy, which must be provided for in all aspects of ministry. (Point out other types of service where fees are applicable.)

The home-grown leaflet should give clear information, describe all the choices available and provide a statement of fees. It is worth stating that all Anglican churches charge fees according to a nationally agreed scale.

These issues require planning in terms of approach and a pastoral commitment to help couples come to a clear understanding of their own situation and responsibilities.

Personal contact and teaching

All such situations are best dealt with personally. Often a simple matter such as not being eligible in one parish is best resolved by the minister telephoning the neighbouring parish to arrange contact. The personal touch is sometimes difficult for busy clergy and is often managed through special 'office hours', but couples should always be helped to feel that this enquiry is just as important to the Church as it is to them. One good idea is to hold an annual meeting for all those with forthcoming wedding dates, providing tea, cake and initial information. Members of the parish ministry team and congregation can be present to share their insights and couples can be encouraged to share their own plans and expectations. A visit to the church building itself provides an opportunity to root the moment and affords a setting for prayer, the reading of Scripture and perhaps even the exchange of the Peace. Practical arrangements can be discussed and common concerns laid to rest. This is a good way of showing that marriage in church is valued by others in society and by the Church. Personal contact is made and a lot of telephoning is avoided.

When an interview is arranged, be prepared. Engaged couples are full of enthusiasm and seem to have the habit of arriving early! Have examples of the service to hand and resources for choosing hymns and music. Once again, many parishes produce drafts of specimen readings and hymns for couples to take away and ponder. Generally speaking, it is best to try and separate interviews that have administration as the focus from times of teaching. Sometimes a brief meeting is all that is required to make choices over flowers, choir, bells and so on, whilst a longer time can be spent working through the Marriage Service word by word as a way of teaching the Christian understanding of marriage in the Anglican tradition. The temptation here is to start discussing who stands where and when to sit or stand, but these are matters best kept for the rehearsal. I find couples really value sitting down with a priest and working through what they will hear, say and sing so that they understand the meaning and spiritual depth of the service. In many ways, this is an opportunity of turning a service into a sacramental moment, full of value and grace. This meeting is best ended with prayer, especially if going into church is possible, so that couples can feel the closeness of God at such a special time in their lives.

Other helpful ideas include:

- presenting a copy of the Marriage Service as a wedding present from the church to be kept with the wedding photographs;

- telling couples that the church will remember them in prayer on their first anniversary;

- encouraging the couple to come to a Sunday service immediately before their wedding day when they will be prayed for by name in the intercessions.

The rehearsal

The rehearsal is a very important time. It is good to remember that it is not the wedding itself and that couples are merely walking through the service rather than trying to remember what to do. That is the task of the presiding minister on the day. Rehearsals should be times of encouragement, fun and confidence building. The priest is there on the day to enable the exchange of vows, not to burden the couple with ritual tasks. The rehearsal is a liberating exercise so that in the midst of all the wonderful trimmings of a wedding, the couple can focus, however briefly, on the importance of their commitment to each other.

At a rehearsal couples should be encouraged to:

- dress down for the occasion, coming casual as a contrast to the real thing;

- invite key participants along as well as family members (so long as spectators do not detract from the rehearsal or force it to be rushed);

- say out loud all that they will say out loud at the wedding;

- ask any question that may be a cause of concern.

Rehearsals are good times for briefing ushers and family photographers or video amateurs. It is also a good idea to receive the copies of the order of service (if there is one) so that these cannot be forgotten on the day.

Many will agree that good preparation is the key to an honest and meaningful celebration of marriage in church. Couples in love need clergy to love them through such an important event. In the preparation for a marriage service, clergy are called to best practice and to model the Good Shepherd as a pattern for ministry and witness for the world.

Such ministry continues in the years to come. A new aspect of the Notes in the *Common Worship* Marriage Service is the explicit reference to the future role of clergy and the ministry of the whole Church, 'to be available for counselling and support in the years that follow'. Parishes often fail to keep records of marriages that can be easily accessed so as to send anniversary cards or invitations to church services with ease. Keeping in contact has a powerful effect on couples and shows, at least, that the Church values its own contribution to their marriage and is still available for them. Recently I heard of a good example that is typical of many other experiences. Having married an 'average' couple, who were sympathetic to the Church but did not attend worship, one parish continued to send an anniversary card for the first five years of married life. On the fourth anniversary, following the delivery of one such card, the husband turned up at the vicarage, visibly distressed, asking for a quick word with the vicar. The wife was sitting outside in their car, too anxious to come in herself. After lots of tears, it transpired that the couple had been struggling to conceive their first child and were hesitating about starting fertility treatment for fear of breaking some ecclesiastical rule. After careful listening and pastoral advice, the husband left the vicarage to rejoin his wife with the resolve to find the best solution for themselves as a couple. Three months later, with the pressure released, the couple conceived naturally and a year later they were knocking on the vicarage door again, seeking not marriage or counselling but a baptism! If only pastoral care was always this effective and immediate! Nevertheless it does show that the Church has a continuing commitment and responsibility for the people it joins in marriage. Many different pastoral situations arise and it is by no means always possible to be informed or available, but to offer such support is to embody our belief that marriage is for better or for worse, lifelong and holy.

2 The Marriage Service: Using the new liturgy

Before the service

The assumption that effective preparation takes place before a marriage service is shown in the new service by the Notes and by a new Pastoral Introduction to the rite (reproduced overleaf). Inspired by a text in *A New Zealand Prayer Book*, it offers a brief rationale for the celebration of marriage in church. It is not intended to be read aloud but to be printed in the order of service and read by the congregation before the service begins. This may be desirable but it presumes that there is such an order. However, many weddings take place with hymn books only being distributed to the people. Already many have found it helpful to use this prologue in a public way so as to help the congregation prepare for the entry of the bride or couple together. If used in this way it can be personalized with the names of the bride and groom and can even include another voice for the passage from 1 Corinthians.

This time before the service should be used to deliver any practical notices, so that such announcements do not disrupt the flow of the liturgy. There is nothing worse than the entry of the bride being followed by instructions about confetti and directions to the lavatory. People value knowing what is the right and what is the wrong thing to do in a particular church building and its surroundings. Even those unfamiliar with church seem to react better to clear, friendly, firm instructions. This also often applies to over-zealous photographers and people with video cameras.

THE MARRIAGE SERVICE
This may be read by those present before the service begins.

A wedding is one of life's great moments, a time of solemn commitment as well as good wishes, feasting and joy. St John tells us how Jesus shared in such an occasion at Cana, and gave there a sign of new beginnings as he turned water into wine.

Marriage is intended by God to be a creative relationship, as his blessing enables husband and wife to love and support each other in good times and in bad, and to share in the care and upbringing of children. For Christians, marriage is also an invitation to share life together in the spirit of Jesus Christ. It is based upon a solemn, public and life-long covenant between a man and a woman, declared and celebrated in the presence of God and before witnesses.

On this their wedding day the bride and groom face each other, make their promises and receive God's blessing. You are witnesses of the marriage, and express your support by your presence and your prayers. Your support does not end today: the couple will value continued encouragement in the days and years ahead of them.

Love is patient; love is kind; love is not envious or boastful or arrogant or rude. It does not insist on its own way; it is not irritable or resentful; it does not rejoice in wrongdoing, but rejoices in the truth. It bears all things, believes all things, hopes all things, endures all things.

1 Corinthians 13.4-7

Coaching the people

It may also be valuable before the service to coach the congregation on various aspects of the service and to explain the flow of what is to take place. This coaching may well include a brief explanation of the role of the congregation:

- being there to support the couple through prayer and singing;

- acting as general witnesses of the marriage;

- and sharing in the couple's commitment to each other by looking forward to the years ahead.

A brief description of the main parts of the service can also be useful:

- entry, consent, readings, exchange of vows, exchange of rings, intercession, registration, blessing and so on.

This is a time to instil confidence in a congregation so that participation is optimum.

Don't panic!

Immediately before the service is a tense time and things do sometimes go wrong. I well remember one bride who arrived with veil firmly down because she had contracted chicken pox. If that was not enough to make the occasion memorable, she announced during the first hymn that the large bow on the back of her dress had come unattached. Not unduly concerned, I was then informed that her dress did not meet in the middle at the back and so the removal of the bow would reveal more to the congregation than might be appropriate for this particular moment of the wedding experience. Swift instructions about where the vestry was and the help of a bridesmaid meant that decorum was maintained. Whatever may be amiss, it is the task of the presiding minister to remain calm and confident and to enable the couple to feel confident in the ministry of the Church at all times.

'Here comes the bride . . .'

Meeting the bride is an important moment. Do not forget to greet the groom on the way to the bride, perhaps by an encouraging word and a handshake. If it is possible to welcome the bride through the grandest door of the church this is desirable as well as full of significance. It may or may not be the most commonly used entrance but this door of the church is the portal through which all important rites of passage quite literally pass. In a traditional church building the west door often represents the symbolic entrance into God's presence or the entry into glory. Highly decorated west fronts such as those of Wells Cathedral and Salisbury Cathedral show us the traditional understanding of this moment of entrance. However, where it is impossible to use such doors, an understanding of the symbolism will ensure that a suitable entrance is available in every place. At the end of the service the married couple should also leave by the main door if possible.

It is fully acceptable for the couple to choose to enter church together if they wish. This will be new to many but is a welcome option. Increasingly couples view their marriage as the sealing of an already existing relationship and less as a joining of two separate individuals. The equality of entrance is also an attractive action to mirror the equality of commitment in words soon to come. Couples should be given the opportunity to make an informed choice about this moment and supported in their decision.

Practical matters

During the welcoming of the bride or couple at the door photographs should be kept to a minimum. When the minister has checked that the bride is ready and does not require any immediate assistance, the appropriate signal to the organist starts the procession. No matter how ancient or modern the church building, the entry procession should be dignified and slow. It is an important moment for all concerned. Careful rehearsal will ensure the bridal party (groom, best man, bridesmaids, page boys etc.) take their appropriate places. If the bride and groom have entered separately, they should have the opportunity to greet each other, however briefly. It is especially good if space in the church allows the couple to be seen from behind by the people, with attendants fanning out on either side.

The Marriage Service

The structure of the service

Introduction

The Welcome

Preface

The Declarations

The Collect

Readings

Sermon

The Marriage

The Vows

The Giving of Rings

The Proclamation

The Blessing of the Marriage

Registration of the Marriage

Prayers

The Dismissal

As with all the *Common Worship* material, the service begins with a clear outline of the service. These headings are used throughout the printed text itself. This is a principle of all the new services that shows the importance of structure and shape. Structure is important so that the service has a clear beginning and ending, and incorporates all the main components for a particular liturgical celebration. Shape is important so that the purpose of the rite is clearly shown in what is going on. Here we see a clear structure, identifying the various parts of the marriage service in their recommended order and the clear shape of two sections, representing the inherent nature of marriage services both in history and practice. This description can be used as a teaching aid in preparation so that couples can see an overview of what is happening in the service.

The type of church building and the layout of its furniture will always dictate the movement within a service to some extent. In most churches the traditional pattern of greeting at the door, marrying at the chancel step and praying and blessing in the sanctuary will be the preferred option. The structure of the service reflects this pattern. However, it is also possible for couples to choose alternative patterns:

- the bride may be escorted by another member of the family rather than her father;

- having friends or family gather around in place of traditional attendants;

- the couple may sit facing the congregation for part of the service;

- the traditional ceremony of 'Giving Away' is optional (Note 6);

- the bride and bridegroom may choose to have their parents declare their affirmation of the intention to marry (Note 6).

The minister should be aware of what the church building is 'saying' to the couple and utilize its best potential for the celebration of the rite. Church buildings may require imaginative use to enable profound liturgical celebration. Furniture may need to be rearranged for weddings so as to provide good space for couple and attendants. Perhaps some form of temporary staging will be required so that couples can be seen more clearly. It may even be necessary to perform the whole service in front of the screen if it is a barrier to good visibility. Informal advice on the use of churches for marriages and other liturgical occasions can be obtained from a diocesan liturgical committee or team.

Introduction

The couple and the people remain standing until after the Collect.

The Welcome

The minister 'welcomes the people', and the first words spoken do need to sound welcoming. If informal words are used, this welcome should include the names of the couple and possibly the previously mentioned description of the role of the congregation. Wedding congregations are notorious for poor response – many clergy find funeral congregations easier to work with – so good encouragement is needed. Other appropriate words may be used but the Grace is provided here as a formula familiar to church people and others. The major advantage of the Grace is that it can stand alone and need not necessarily require the response 'and also with you' if it is likely to be unforthcoming. The minister will need to judge whether or not the congregation contains enough churchgoers to elicit a response or whether to include this part of the service in any coaching before the service begins. If there is to be a printed order of service the Grace will be printed to encourage a confident response.

> The grace of our Lord Jesus Christ,
> the love of God,
> and the fellowship of the Holy Spirit
> be with you all
> **and also with you.**

The sentence from the First Letter of John is optional.

> God is love, and those who live in love live in God
> and God lives in them.

The next prayer (see overleaf) fulfils the function of a prayer of preparation. In it we acknowledge that God is the source of many wonderful things and without him our efforts, even on a wedding day, are 'worth nothing'. The second part asks God to send his Spirit to inspire the participants to worship and service with willing minds and thankful hearts. The words of this prayer offer a framework for an address at a marriage service, especially if the people have indeed said it together. The prayer is entirely optional and although printed in bold type may be spoken by the priest alone. It is drawn from the Church of Scotland's *Book of Common Order*.

Another possibility, suggested by the words of the prayer, is that the first part may be said by the priest, the second part by priest and people together. Inviting the people to join in the prayer assumes two things: first, that they have the text available to them and second, that they will make a strong enough response. If in doubt, it is better to briefly describe the meaning of a prayer and then for it to be said on behalf of the congregation, rather than cruise on regardless or strive for good responses from a shy congregation.

> **God of wonder and of joy:**
> **grace comes from you,**
> **and you alone are the source of life and love.**
> **Without you, we cannot please you;**
> **without your love, our deeds are worth nothing.**
> **Send your Holy Spirit,**
> **and pour into our hearts**
> **   that most excellent gift of love,**
> **that we may worship you now**
> **with thankful hearts**
> **and serve you always with willing minds;**
> **through Jesus Christ our Lord.**
> **Amen.**

The Preface

The section entitled 'The Introduction' in the ASB has now been entitled 'Preface', which more accurately describes the context of these words. It provides a rationale for the marriage. This new text is marginally shorter than the slightly altered ASB form which is also given as an alternative in the Supplementary Texts. The wording of the new text is judged to be more accessible to non-churchgoers. Such findings were products of the exhaustive process of experimentation and consultation with over eight hundred parishes that used the draft material before final revision and authorization. The Preface provided in the main text of the service had been placed in an appendix but was found to be more popular. Both these texts can be read with enthusiastic drama and deliberate pauses at each paragraph.

The new text differs from the previous and now alternative preface in the following ways. This listing includes changes made to the texts during the revision process.

Paragraph 1

i)   The first line becomes explicitly Trinitarian.

ii)   We pray for God's blessing rather than to ask for it.

iii) 'To celebrate their love' is a reference that can resonate with the congregation, who will be looking forward to the reception.

iv) The reference to the wedding in Cana of Galilee is moved to the fourth paragraph so as not to come out of the blue as in the previous provision.

Paragraph 2

v) The reference to the Bible is omitted.

vi) Difficult words and images such as 'holy mystery' and 'one flesh' are omitted. Man and woman now grow together in love and trust, recognizing that this is the beginning of a life-long journey which will involve heart, body and mind.

Paragraph 3

vii) This gift from God is instrumental in bringing the couple together.

viii) Sexual union and lifelong commitment are paired. The words 'sexual union' are preferred to the ASB's rather coy 'bodily union', as being more frank and straightforward.

ix) This gift and this pairing are explicitly seen as the foundation of family life and involve all those included or potentially included as family members.

Paragraph 4

This is more explicit about why reference is made to the wedding at Cana in the Gospel story. By his presence with those celebrating their new relationship Jesus blessed marriage and blesses us today who come to begin this way of life made holy by God.

x) The reason for referring to the wedding at Cana is made more clear; Jesus was involved in such a celebration as the congregation now present are witnessing.

xi) The word 'belong' is omitted.

xii) The previous list of reasons for marriage – negative rather than positive – is turned into a less threatening pairing with the emphasis on a responsible decision.

Paragraph 5

xiii) The couple are named at the beginning of the final paragraph.

xiv) The reference to joining hands is omitted.

xv) Clear statements such as 'we pray' are preferred to longer-winded phrases beginning 'therefore'.

The giving of the two rings is now commonplace so 'each' is included in brackets for omission when only one ring is to be used.

In the presence of God, Father, Son and Holy Spirit
we have come together
to witness the marriage of N and N,
to pray for God's blessing on them,
to share in their joy
and to celebrate their love.

Marriage is a gift of God in creation
through which husband and wife may know the grace of
    God.
It is given
that as man and woman grow together in love and trust,
they shall be united with one another in heart, body and
    mind,
as Christ is united with his bride, the Church.

The gift of marriage brings husband and wife together
in the delight and tenderness of sexual union
and joyful commitment to the end of their lives.
It is given as the foundation of family life
in which children are [born and] nurtured
and in which each member of the family,
in good times and in bad,
may find strength, companionship and comfort,
and grow to maturity in love.

Marriage is a way of life made holy by God,
and blessed by the presence of our Lord Jesus Christ
with those celebrating a wedding at Cana in Galilee.
Marriage is a sign of unity and loyalty
which all should uphold and honour.
It enriches society and strengthens community.
No one should enter into it lightly or selfishly
but reverently and responsibly in the sight of almighty God.

N and N are now to enter this way of life.
They will each give their consent to the other
and make solemn vows,
and in token of this they will [each] give and receive a ring.
We pray with them that the Holy Spirit will guide and
    strengthen them,
that they may fulfil God's purposes
for the whole of their earthly life together.

The Alternative Preface is provided in the Supplementary Texts and contains a few minor changes to the ASB text.

i)   'Scriptures' has been replaced by 'the Bible' to avoid any confusion with the writings of other faiths.

ii) The reference to children is reworded in accordance with the new Preface so as to be pastorally sensitive to those who cannot have children or who are of 'riper years'. Whilst it is recognized in the wider social context that marriage is the relationship that is most appropriate for childbirth and a safe environment for the nurture of children, such a reference is not necessarily specific to the couple coming for marriage. Family life is given rightful prominence.

iii) 'Nurture' has been preferred to 'brought up' so as to allow for existing and adopted children.

iv) 'Weighing the consequences' has been replaced by 'reverently, responsibly, and after serious thought'. This is a change to early drafts of the new text, not to the ASB provision.

We have come together in the presence of God, to witness the marriage of N and N, to ask his blessing on them, and to share in their joy. Our Lord Jesus Christ was himself a guest at a wedding in Cana of Galilee, and through his Spirit he is with us now.

The Bible teaches us that marriage is a gift of God in creation and means of his grace, a holy mystery in which man and woman become one flesh. It is God's purpose that, as husband and wife give themselves to each other in love throughout their lives, they shall be united in that love as Christ is united with his Church.

Marriage is given, that husband and wife may comfort and help each other, living faithfully together in need and in plenty, in sorrow and in joy. It is given, that with delight and tenderness they may know each other in love, and, through the joy of their bodily union, may strengthen the union of their hearts and lives. It is given as the foundation of family life in which children may be born and nurtured in accordance with God's will, to his praise and glory.

In marriage husband and wife belong to one another, and they begin a new life together in the community. It is a way of life that all should honour; and it must not be undertaken carelessly, lightly, or selfishly, but reverently, responsibly, and after serious thought.

This is the way of life, created and hallowed by God, that N and N are now to begin. They will each give their consent to the other; they will join hands and exchange solemn vows, and in token of this they will [each] give and receive a ring.

Therefore, on this their wedding day we pray with them, that, strengthened and guided by God, they may fulfil his purpose for the whole of their earthly life together.

The Declarations

First comes a question to the congregation as a preliminary to the declaration by bride and bridegroom.

The minister says to the congregation

First, I am required to ask anyone present who knows a reason why these persons may not lawfully marry, to declare it now.

This moment of uncomfortable squirming is the subject of much folklore and anxiety. Objections hardly ever arise and can be received only if either the bride or bridegroom is:

1. under the legal age for marriage;

2. not a British citizen (unless the proper permission has been given for the marriage of a foreign national);

3. too closely related;

4. currently married to a living partner.

I have never had such an objection happen in a wedding but it always seems to happen on television! Couples can be anxious about this moment, especially if friends have jokingly threatened to say something. If a serious or flippant objection is made publicly, the response of the presiding minister needs to be clear and unambiguous.

1. Ask the congregation to be seated if they are standing.

2. Seat the couple and reassure them.

3. Ask the objector to join you in the vestry immediately to ascertain the validity of the objection (proof must be given). It is helpful to have another witness present, such as a verger or choir member.

4. Ask the organist to play while this takes place.

5. Either, return to continue the service, stating that the objection is invalid (the objector may need to be asked to leave the church).

6. Or, if the objection is judged to be valid, the bride and groom must be brought into the vestry to ascertain if this is the case.

7. The minister makes a final judgement and the service proceeds or not.

It is remarkable that I can find no procedure laid down to advise clergy on the handling of this potentially disastrous situation, other than in the *Guide to the Law* referred to in Chapter 5. Nor do I remember any training for such an eventuality. What is clear though, is that if the couple have both signed the usual Banns of Marriage application form and provided a genuine Banns Certificate from another parish (if appropriate), or if the appropriate licence has been obtained, then the minister is acting in good faith and the service should go ahead. Any irregularity later discovered to exist will then need to be investigated by others in authority.

The moment that the minister speaks directly to the bride and bridegroom for the first time has a certain poignancy. It quickens the emotions in the couple and prefigures the first responses from them, which are about to be spoken. These words should be audible to the whole congregation but eye contact with the couple is important. This section has a dual purpose: it first states that these vows are to be made in the presence of God and are therefore holy and important, then immediately warns that it is now that any legal reasons against the marriage should be declared. In the preparation for this service it is often useful to use this text as an opportunity for openness and honesty between the couple so that any past misdemeanours can be forgiven before these words are spoken on their great day, even though it strictly relates only to legal impediments to marriage.

The minister says to the couple

The vows you are about to take are to be made in the presence of God,
who is judge of all and knows all the secrets of our hearts;
therefore if either of you knows a reason why you may not lawfully marry, you must declare it now.

Next the minister speaks to the bride or bridegroom personally. There it is important to have discovered beforehand what form of names the couple would like used during the service. Some may choose their full set of Christian names, or just their first name, or the abbreviation by which they are generally known. It is important that it is the couple who decide this together. This is also the first time the bride and bridegroom will have spoken out loud in the service. They should be encouraged to be firm and audible – the general principle being that if they speak at a volume that seems slightly too loud for them it is probably just right for the congregation to hear.

The minister says to the bridegroom

N, will you take *N* to be your wife?
Will you love her, comfort her, honour her and protect her,
and, forsaking all others,
be faithful to her as long as you both shall live?

He answers
I will.

The identical question is repeated to the bride, although the Notes also allow the question to be put to the bride first and then to the groom.

One of the new features of this service is an address to the congregation after these personal and individual declarations by the couple, requesting a declaration from the people. It comes from the Service of Dedication after Civil Marriage and has been widely welcomed; this can be a great moment for congregation and couple alike. The response, 'We will', is brief enough to be coached before the service even if a printed order is not available. The very brave may like the couple to turn and face the people at this point. This support from family and friends can find its parallel in the ordination service, where before the Ordination Prayer the congregation promises to support candidates. This is a significant statement for couple and congregation alike and contains a whole raft of meanings, ranging from emotional support to prayer and practical help. There is a tension throughout this new service between allowing the words and

actions to flow and commenting on the meaning to enable greater
understanding and participation. Balance is required as too many
informal but educative words can interrupt the liturgical flow.
However, this is one moment when an informal introduction can
increase the awareness of the value of this response. Such
informal words can reflect upon the similar commitment made by
the couple and the fact that this marriage involves all present
rather than just the couple themselves. The key pairing of words
is 'support and uphold', 'now and in the years to come'.

The minister says to the congregation

Will you, the families and friends of N and N,
support and uphold them in their marriage
    now and in the years to come?
All **We will.**

The Collect

The invitation to prayer needs careful handling. There are still
people who when invited, 'Let us pray', will drop to their knees.
The correct liturgical posture for this prayer is standing. The
minister needs to introduce the prayer with a suitable description
that will lead the people into a time of silence before saying the
Collect. Informal but thought-out words are the most
appropriate.

God our Father,
from the beginning,
you have blessed creation with abundant life.
Pour out your blessings upon N and N,
that they may be joined in mutual love and companionship,
in holiness, and in commitment to each other.
We ask this through our Lord Jesus Christ your Son,
who is alive and reigns with you,
in the unity of the Holy Spirit,
one God, now and for ever.
All **Amen.**

Readings

Too often, the marriage service has avoided the proclamation of Scripture. Here a proper Liturgy of the Word is implied, and Note 5 demands that at least one reading from the Bible must be used. Suggested readings are available on pages 82–5 of this book. If occasion demands, either the Sermon or the Readings and Sermon may come after the Blessing of the Marriage. At either point, it is good for the people to be seated and for the couple to be seated on two chairs in view of the congregation.

Sermon

One priest I knew always used to preach the same sermon at every wedding, using the same illustrations but, thankfully, remembering to change the names of the bride and bridegroom. The choir and servers knew the sermon off by heart, as did some of the couples themselves. It was a standing joke. Whilst most clergy will use familiar phrases and have a selection of key points to share as a response to each individual situation, such repetition is to be avoided. Local small talk will soon devalue a wedding address that is always the same or always uses the same illustrations. Yet, the opportunity for effective preaching is easily lost upon a congregation that is perhaps unused to hearing sermons, no matter how good the sermon is. The sermon is therefore a good opportunity for more informal words which can make each service personal to every couple and should reflect theologically on the reading(s) and the meaning of Christian marriage. At this point brevity is often a virtue.

The Marriage

> *The couple stand before the minister. A hymn may be sung.*

It is probably best for the congregation to sit after standing for a hymn, so that the couple and their attendants may be seen and so that the action of standing can accompany the proclamation of the marriage to come later.

The Vows

> *The minister introduces the vows in these or similar words*
>
> N and N, I now invite you to join hands and make your vows, in the presence of God and his people.

Note 6 provides for the traditional ceremony of 'Giving Away'. Most will still value this moment and many will also value the now explicit options available for making this act more pastorally flexible. Immediately before the couple exchange vows, the minister may ask: 'Who brings this woman to be married to this man?' It is worth noting the change in wording here. The word 'gives' is replaced by 'brings'. This shows a better understanding of what is taking place: the family bring a woman to her marriage, rather than give her as a commodity. The bride's father (or mother, or another member of her family, or a friend representing the family) presents the bride's right hand to the minister who places it in the bridegroom's right hand.

Alternatively, and as a different expression of family support and of 'handing over' to a new relationship, after the bride and bridegroom have made their Declarations, the minister may address the parents of bride and bridegroom in these or similar words. With careful preparation these options can help couples through often complicated family concerns such as when there is no father to give away the bride or when there is family opposition to the marriage. It can also be used when there is a rift between the respective parents of the couple. In such cases, careful consultation is required with the couple before any presumption is made about an explicit presentation of this moment as a sign of new-found family unity.

> N and N have declared their intention towards each other.
> As their parents,
> will you now entrust your son and daughter to one another
> as they come to be married?
>
> *Both sets of parents respond:*
> We will.

In the vows, it should be understood that both the spoken word and action form the vow made one to another. Facing towards each other and holding right hands are important signs of the joining of two people in marriage. The vows are identical for male and female.

The decision over which vow is appropriate for each couple will be made in the marriage preparation. Once again, the bride may make her vow first so as not to model a pecking order between genders or any outdated understanding of ownership or pre-eminence of the man in the marriage relationship. Two forms of vow are permitted. First the main text, which omits the promise to obey.

> I, N, take you, N,
> to be my wife/husband,
> to have and to hold
> from this day forward;
> for better, for worse,
> for richer, for poorer,
> in sickness and in health,
> to love and to cherish,
> till death us do part;
> according to God's holy law.
> In the presence of God I make this vow.

See how the final line of the vow has changed significantly. 'And this is my solemn vow' becomes 'In the presence of God I make this vow.' The emphasis is on God's presence and on the personal commitment to the vow. I believe this new provision to be one of the best improvements in the new service.

There are three common ways of making marriage vows. First, the individual repeats the vow after the minister in short phrases that can be easily recalled. This is the most common method.

Advantages: fewer mistakes; couples can look at each other.

Disadvantages: involves a third voice; couples may concentrate on the words they are having to repeat rather than on their meaning; there is a temptation to look at the minister rather than the marriage partner.

Second, couples read their vows so as to make them have a confident flow. This requires a large print version, laminated or on card and held by the minister or the individual.

Advantages: the vows flow smoothly and are uninterrupted.

Disadvantages: the vows can sound too 'read'; eye contact is difficult.

Third, the vows can be learned by heart.

Advantages: spiritually and emotionally moving if successful; offers the opportunity to reflect on the words in the process of memorization.

Disadvantages: disappointing if unsuccessful; often a cause of great anxiety; it is important to have the above-mentioned printed text as a back-up.

Mistakes occasionally happen. Usually, the simple answer is to repeat a line so that the person feels they have made a well-spoken vow to their partner. I remember one wedding when it appeared to the congregation that I married the groom myself, having read the words of the vow to be repeated and because the bride was weeping (with happiness) so much that she could not get the words out coherently. I'm sure that we've all been happy ever after! Surely the bottom line here is that the couple are given enough confidence to say their vows in the manner of their choosing so that it is, to them and all present, full of the sincerity the words imply. Couples must leave church feeling they have made their vows well.

In the Supplementary Texts, Alternative Vows Form 2 is the BCP version (see Note 7) which includes the word 'obey'.

I, N, take thee, N, to my wedded wife, to have and to hold from this day forward, for better for worse, for richer for poorer, in sickness and in health, to love and to cherish, till death us do part, according to God's holy ordinance; and thereto I plight thee my troth.

The next version provides an option to omit the word 'obey'.

> I, N, take thee, N, to my wedded husband, to have and to hold from this day forward, for better for worse, for richer for poorer, in sickness and in health, to love, cherish, and to obey, till death us do part, according to God's holy ordinance; and thereto I give thee my troth.

The exchange of vows is in many ways the climax of the service and needs sensitive leadership by the minister. Couples should be rehearsed to listen carefully to the minister and encouraged to speak audibly. It is quite acceptable to practise vows in full at the rehearsal.

The Giving of Rings

> *The minister receives the ring(s), and says . . .*
>
> Heavenly Father, by your blessing,
> let *these rings* be to N and N
> a symbol of unending love and faithfulness,
> to remind them of the vow and covenant
> which they have made this day
> through Jesus Christ our Lord.
> **Amen.**

Rings are often received from the best man, who needs to have been coached so as to be able to provide them discreetly. In the church I grew up in, there was always a fear that the rings would be dropped down the heating grate so the best man needed to be positioned carefully. Placing them on the flat page of the minister's book is the best way of handing the rings from person to person. There are no words for the best man to speak at this point. Another possibility is for one ring to be presented by each side of the two families or one by the best man and one by a bridesmaid. It is always difficult when very small children are asked to carry in the rings on a cushion. Bitter experience recalls that it is probably best if the rings are attached in some temporary way and that the cushion (if used) is placed somewhere safe on arrival at the place where the exchange of rings is to take place.

An alternative prayer is offered in the Supplementary Texts and is derived from Eastern rites, drawing on imagery from the Song of Songs and 1 Corinthians.

Heavenly Father, source of everlasting love,
revealed to us in Jesus Christ
    and poured into our hearts through your Holy Spirit;
that love which many waters cannot quench,
    neither the floods drown;
that love which is patient and kind, enduring all things
    without end;
by your blessing, let these rings be to N and N
symbols to remind them of the covenant made this day
through your grace in the love of your Son
and in the power of your Spirit.

All **Amen.**

Note 8 gives the option for bride and bridegroom to say together the words that accompany the exchange of rings to mark the equality of the action. It may be necessary to exchange rings before speaking together if this option is taken. The same possibilities for repeating or saying these words apply as at the vows.

N, I give you this ring
as a sign of our marriage.
With my body I honour you,
all that I am I give to you,
and all that I have I share with you,
within the love of God,
Father, Son and Holy Spirit.

The Proclamation

The minister addresses the people

Whilst there is no rubric providing instruction, the minister may now invite the congregation to stand, thus lending an action to the words of proclamation; or this may be saved until after the Blessing of the Marriage.

In the presence of God, and before this congregation,
N and N have given their consent
and made their marriage vows to each other.
They have declared their marriage by the joining of hands
and by the giving and receiving of *rings*.
I therefore proclaim that they are husband and wife.

The minister joins their right hands together and says

Those whom God has joined together let no one put
asunder.

The minister may choose, when joining right hands together, to wrap a stole (that is being worn) around the hands of the couple as a sign of sealing the new marriage. This is where the popular phrase 'tying the knot' comes from, and is a useful teaching opportunity for the marriage preparation, especially when discussing traditional phrases that still hold significance today. An alternative action would be to place the minister's hands around the joined hands of the couple.

It is correct that this section, when the couple have been the primary ministers to each other, should conclude here, before the service moves on to the nuptial blessing, at which the priest ministers. So far the couple have done everything: consent and commitment. Now the ministry of the Church takes on a new role of intercession, blessing and, on behalf of the state, registration. In marriage services, the couple minister to each other as they will continue to do throughout their life together. Once again this subtle but important point can be usefully made in preparing for the service.

The Blessing of the Marriage

The ASB relegated the nuptial blessing to the section of additional prayers and it was often omitted. In the *Common Worship* service there are six options, one in the main text and five in the Supplementary Texts. Option 5 incorporates the

Acclamations, which may be added to any of the other blessings or used independently. It will be good for couples to have all these options made available to them so that they can make valuable decisions about which prayer best reflects their understanding of their relationship to each other and to God. Rather than delving into the deeper theological perspectives of each prayer, it is likely that many couples will base their choice on style, length and the pictorial nature of each prayer.

The husband and wife kneel. The minister may use the following blessing or one of those in the Supplementary Texts.

Blessed are you, O Lord our God,
for you have created joy and gladness,
pleasure and delight, love, peace and fellowship.
Pour out the abundance of your blessing
upon N and N in their new life together.
Let their love for each other be a seal upon their hearts,
and a crown upon their heads.
Bless them in their work and in their companionship;
awake and asleep,
in joy and in sorrow,
in life and in death.
Finally, in your mercy, bring them to that banquet
where your saints feast for ever in your heavenly home.
We ask this through Jesus Christ your Son, our Lord,
who lives and reigns with you and the Holy Spirit,
one God, now and for ever.

All **Amen.**

There are five more alternative blessings.

I
God of life and beginnings,
you created man and woman in your likeness
and joined them together in union of body and heart;
God of love and forgiveness,
you loved us in Jesus Christ
who humbled himself to death on a cross;

God of grace and strength,
you bring your people to faith
and fill them with your presence.
Blessed are you, O Lord our God,
for you have created joy and gladness,
pleasure and delight, love, peace and fellowship.
Pour out the abundance of your blessing
upon N and N in their new life together.
Let their love for each other be a seal upon their hearts,
and a crown upon their heads.
Bless them in their work and in their companionship;
awake and asleep,
in joy and in sorrow,
in life and in death.
Finally, in your mercy, bring them to that banquet
where your saints feast for ever in your heavenly home;
we ask this through Jesus Christ your Son, our Lord,
who lives and reigns with you and the Holy Spirit,
one God, now and for ever.
All **Amen.**

2

All praise and blessing to you, God of love,
creator of the universe,
maker of man and woman in your likeness,
source of blessing for married life.
All praise to you, for you have created
  courtship and marriage,
  joy and gladness,
  feasting and laughter,
  pleasure and delight.
May your blessing come in full upon N and N.
May they know your presence
in their joys and in their sorrows.
May they reach old age in the company of friends
and come at last to your eternal kingdom,
through Jesus Christ our Lord.
All **Amen.**

3

Eternal God,
you create us out of love
that we should love you and one another.
Bless this man and this woman, made in your image,
who today become a sign of your faithful love to us
in Christ our Lord.

All **Amen.**

By your Holy Spirit,
fill bride and bridegroom with wisdom and hope
that they may delight in your gift of marriage
and enrich one another in love and faithfulness;
through Jesus Christ our Lord.

All **Amen.**

Bring them to that table
where your saints celebrate for ever in your heavenly home;
through Jesus Christ our Lord,
who with you and the Holy Spirit lives and reigns,
one God, for ever and ever.

All **Amen.**

4

Blessed are you, Lord our God,
God of love, creator of all.

All **Blessed be God for ever.**

Bridegroom Blessed are you, Lord our God,
you make us in your image and likeness.

All **Blessed be God for ever.**

Bride Blessed are you, Lord our God,
you make man and woman to reflect your glory.

All **Blessed be God for ever.**

Bridegroom Blessed are you, Lord our God,
you make us for joy and promise us life.

All **Blessed be God for ever.**

Bride Blessed are you, Lord our God,
you create a people to know your love.

All **Blessed be God for ever.**

Minister	May N and N enjoy the blessing of your kingdom
	Give them faith and joy in their marriage.
	Blessed are you, Lord our God,
	you give joy to bride and groom.
All	**Blessed be God for ever.**
	May their love be fruitful
	and their home a place of peace.
	Blessed are you, Lord our God,
	you make marriage a sign of your love.
All	**Blessed be God for ever.**
	May they know the love of the Father,
	the life of the Son,
	and the joy of the Spirit.
	Blessed are you, Lord our God,
	Lover, Beloved and Friend of Love.
All	**Blessed be God for ever.**

5

Blessed are you, heavenly Father.
All **You give joy to bridegroom and bride.**

Blessed are you, Lord Jesus Christ.
All **You bring life to the world.**

Blessed are you, Holy Spirit of God.
All **You bind us together in love.**

Blessed are you, Father, Son and Holy Spirit, now and
    for ever.
All **Amen.**

The Registration of the Marriage

Note 10 states that the law requires that the registers are filled in immediately after the solemnization of a marriage. This may take place at this point or at the very end of the service. Many will see the advantage of signing at the earlier position so as to be able to continue the service with prayer and end on the high note of the Dismissal. Some will want to separate the Registration from the liturgy itself, so as to keep the work of the state apart from the ministry of the Church. Whichever position is chosen, the Registration requires careful management. The minister should explain, in informal words, what is about to take place.

Registers should always be made up before the service with only the signatures left to complete. It is good to be able to show a register to the participants at the rehearsal as this encourages a greater understanding of their purpose. Ideally, the Registration should take place in full view of the people, rather than hidden from view in a vestry. My own wedding photos show a lovely scene of the two of us signing the register in the vestry with adoring fans looking on – and the sign for the loo in the background.

Signing is an important act in itself and, technically, the marriage is not legal until the Registration has been completed. Hesitations about signing registers in church because it is a secular function are misplaced. Placing it after the blessing of the couple has the advantage of speeding up the signing and keeping the attention of the congregation. This is also a convenient moment for the official photographer to take one or two posed photos, having been made aware beforehand that this must not take more than one or two minutes.

If friends of the couple are playing a piece of music it should have been rehearsed in church and be of sufficient standard so as to edify the whole celebration. This can also be an opportunity for the playing of recorded music. Ministers need to realize that such requests are always sincerely made, certain tracks often holding great meaning for couples. Just because the minister does not recognize the track from Boyzone or Simply Red does not mean it should not be played. However, the rules of good practice apply again – hear the track beforehand, even play it in church to see if the couple are still convinced it works in this setting, and ensure that the audio equipment is adequate for the building. The couple will want this to work as much as the minister.

If the Registration takes place at the end of the service, the traditional act of exchanging partners can be requested. It is advisable for the minister to ascertain previously whether this is wanted, so as to avoid any potential difficulties. The action is symbolic of the joining of two families but is by no means necessary; sensitive decisions can be made, especially when parents of the bride or bridegroom have been divorced or if only one parent is present. When a married couple leaves church after the registration it is a good moment for snap-happy friends to take their pictures. In all, these arrangements should be simple, tidy and confident in order to be successful. A hymn or psalm may follow the signing.

On a practical note, all ministers should be competent in the preparation of registers. If registers are prepared by others, they too should receive good training. A conversation with the Superintendent Registrar is always worthwhile in order to ensure good practice.

Prayers

Note 9 clearly states that several different forms of prayer may be used. An intercession style is provided in the main text and four more in the Supplementary Texts, all but the last including a response. In total, twenty-seven alternative prayers are provided. Free prayer may also be used, including other prayers by the minister. Whatever form the prayer takes, the new service recommends it cover areas of common concern to all.

Thanksgiving
Spiritual growth
Faithfulness, joy, love, forgiveness and healing
Children, other family members and friends

Subjects include: the sharing of love, the home, the Holy Spirit, grace to live well, discipleship, a glimpse of eternal love, the gift of love, marriage as a sign, the joy of loving, the healing of memories, companionship, grace and delight, faithfulness, peace, daily following of Christ, children and home, families, and friends.

Here is a real pastoral opportunity. In my experience in using the draft text, it is quite a moving experience for couples to be able to see all the available prayers, be guided in their choice by the suggested structure, and then choose their own selection. They can take away a copy of the structure and the prayers and often they spend many hours choosing the prayers for their service. Hearing their reasons for their individual choice can tell the minister a lot about their relationship and their family history. The couple can also be given the opportunity to include in prayer the names of any family or friends unable to be present or to mention dead relatives who might be especially missed on such an occasion.

Family and friends can be involved in leading the prayers. The description of the prayers contained in Chapter 4 is given to help ministers help couples with their choices.

> *The prayers conclude with the Lord's Prayer.*

A decision about which authorized version is to be used and whether it is said by all would be normal. The choice is between the ASB version in modern language and the traditional version as commonly used. The couple should join in this decision. A hymn may be sung following the Lord's Prayer.

The Dismissal

The 'you' form in the blessing has been italicized to allow the occasional celebration of marriage by a deacon. The trinitarian form of blessing is highly suitable for the general blessing at a marriage, especially if the new Preface is used, as both make the theological point that the marriage relationship is rooted in the relationship of the Trinity.

> God the Holy Trinity make *you* strong in faith and love,
> defend *you* on every side, and guide *you* in truth and peace;
> and the blessing of God almighty,
> the Father, the Son and the Holy Spirit,
> be among you and remain with you always
> *All* **Amen.**

The Marriage Service within a Celebration of Holy Communion

The structure of the service is as follows:

> **The Gathering**
>
> The Welcome

Prayers of Penitence

Preface

The Declarations

The Collect

The Liturgy of the Word

Readings

Gospel Reading

Sermon

The Marriage

The Vows

The Giving of Rings

The Proclamation

The Blessing of the Marriage

Registration of the Marriage

Prayers

The Liturgy of the Sacrament

The Peace

Preparation of the Table

The Eucharistic Prayer

The Lord's Prayer

The Blessing of the Marriage

Breaking of the Bread

Giving of Communion

Prayer after Communion

The Dismissal

The Marriage Service within a Celebration of Holy Communion
The Notes to the Order for the Celebration of Holy
Communion, as well as the Notes to the Marriage Service,
apply equally to this service. Texts are suggested at different
points, but other suitable texts may be used. Authorized
Prayers of Penitence may be used. In the Liturgy of the Word,
there should be a Gospel reading, preceded by either one or
two other readings from the Bible. If desired, the Blessing of
the Marriage may take place between the Lord's Prayer and
the Breaking of the Bread.

(Note 12 – Notes to the Marriage Service)

The structure of the service

It is convenient that the new-married persons should receive
the Holy Communion at the time of their Marriage, or at
the first opportunity after their Marriage.

The Book of Common Prayer

Thomas Cranmer always intended that marriage should take
place in the context of the Eucharist or that the couple should
receive the sacrament as soon as possible after their marriage.
The joining of souls is given fullest expression in the sharing of
Holy Communion, especially if immediately after the exchange of
solemn vows. The Notes to the Order for the Celebration of
Holy Communion, as well as the Notes to the Marriage Service,
apply equally to this service. A selection of texts is given but
other suitable eucharistic resources may be used, such as seasonal
material. The Liturgy of the Word should include a Gospel
reading, preceded by either one or two other readings from the
Bible. If desired, the Blessing of the Marriage may take place
between the Lord's Prayer and the Breaking of the Bread. Note
11 of the new service looks back to Cranmer's intention.

For communicant members of the Church it is appropriate
that they receive communion soon after their marriage. For
some this may make it appropriate for the marriage to take
place within the context of a Celebration of Holy
Communion.

Once again, the clear structure gives opportunity for imaginative use of buildings. I have heard of one such wedding where the Introduction took place at the door, the Liturgy of the Word took place around the pulpit and lectern, the Marriage took place at the foot of the sanctuary steps and the Liturgy of the Sacrament took place around the altar. This worked particularly well with a modest number of wedding guests, able to move with the couple. In some churches, this structure will also enable a generous use of music. There are also other pastoral opportunities such as the involvement of family members or the couple themselves, especially in the Preparation of the Gifts.

Most extended families have sad or awkward stories of strained relationships or past arguments. The eucharistic material provides opportunities for coming together on a happy day and for family reconciliation. Four areas encourage reconciliation at this point:

- the joy of a new marriage relationship;

- the sharing of the Eucharist;

- the call to penitence;

- the sharing of the Peace.

Elements of the service

Prayers of Penitence

Invitation to Confession

The practice of including a penitential section so close to the beginning of the service will be powerful to some and irksome to others. Each couple will know whether it is right for them to include such material according to their own faith journeys, their time together and family relationships. However, penitential prayers should also be seen as a natural and usual precursor to receiving communion.

> As we prepare to hear God's word
> and to celebrate the marriage of N and N,
> we remember our human frailty
> and our need for God's help in all that we do.
>
> (or)

Gathered together as God's family,
let us ask forgiveness from our heavenly Father,
for he is full of gentleness and compassion.

(or)

We come to God as one from whom no secrets are hidden,
to ask for his forgiveness and peace.

The suggested Confession is explicit in this suggestion. This
prayer is meant to be said by all together but may be said by the
couple alone. It would be easy in such cases to make homiletic
links between 'bind up our wounds' and the 'tying the knot'
moment in the Proclamation.

All **Lord our God,**
  in our sin we have avoided your call.
  Our love for you is like a morning cloud,
  like the dew that goes away early.
  Have mercy on us;
  deliver us from judgement;
  bind up our wounds
  and revive us;
  in Jesus Christ our Lord. Amen.

The Absolution has the *you* and *your* in italics to enable the use
of an *us* form if preferred, as in the Kyrie form of penitence that
is the second option.

The Lord forgive *you your* sin,
  unite *you* in the love which took Christ to the cross,
  and bring *you* in the Spirit to his wedding feast in heaven.
All **Amen.**

  (or)

  Lord, in our weakness you are our strength.
  Lord, have mercy.
All **Lord, have mercy.**

Lord, when we stumble, you raise us up.
Christ, have mercy.
All **Christ, have mercy.**

Lord, when we fail, you give us new life.
Lord, have mercy.
All **Lord, have mercy.**

May God in his goodness forgive us *our* sins,
grant us strength in *our* weakness,
and bring *us* to eternal life,
through Jesus Christ our Lord.
All **Amen.**

The Liturgy of the Word

Gospel Acclamations

These new texts complement possible choices made with a verse
from St Mark for a synoptic choice of Gospel Reading and a
verse from St John for an alternative choice.

Alleluia, alleluia.
God made them male and female
and the two will become one
Alleluia.   *cf Mark 10.8*

(*or*)

Alleluia, alleluia.
God is love;
let us love one another
as God has loved us.
Alleluia.   *cf 1 John 4.8-11*

The Liturgy of the Sacrament

Introduction to the Peace

Part of me says that exchanging the Peace would enhance the
Marriage Service whether or not in the context of the Eucharist.
I am sure that even the unchurched would find this acceptable

after a simple explanation – in fact a wedding might be just the most obvious liturgy for such an act of fellowship. If being used in a non-eucharistic marriage, the Peace might be well placed following the Proclamation or the Blessing of the Marriage or even after the Registration.

To crown all things there must be love.
Let the peace of Christ rule in your hearts.
The peace of the Lord be always with you

All **and also with you.**

(or)

We have celebrated the love of N and N.
We now celebrate God's love for all of us.
Peace, in Christ, to all of you

All **and also with you.**

1 Peter 5.14

Preparation of the Table and the Gifts

This simple action may be accompanied by words to be said by the minister immediately before the Eucharistic Prayer begins. Obviously this is a chance for well-chosen people to bring forward the gifts, perhaps best friends, ushers or representatives from each family. When the couple already have children this is clear opportunity for their involvement. The couple themselves may present the bread and wine.

In your goodness, Lord,
accept the gift of our love,
and with a father's affection watch over this couple
you have joined in the covenant of marriage;
through Jesus Christ our Lord.

All **Amen.**

Prefaces in the Eucharistic Prayer

The Marriage Preface in the Eucharistic Prayer should almost always be used on such an occasion to give the Eucharistic Prayer a flavour of the marriage celebration. The first Proper Preface is from the ASB tradition, whilst the Extended Proper Preface is taken from *A Prayer Book for Australia.* Other prefaces may be used, although not all the Eucharistic Prayers in Order One allow for the use of Proper Prefaces. The Extended Proper Preface (example (b) below) is intended to replace all material between the opening dialogue and the Sanctus, and is suitable for use with Eucharistic Prayers A, B and E in Order One.

Short Proper Preface

And now we give you thanks
because you have made the union between Christ and
    his Church
a pattern for the marriage between husband and wife.
Therefore with angels . . .

Extended Proper Preface

All glory, honour, thanks and praise
be given to you, creator of heaven and earth.
When you made us in your image,
creating us male and female,
you gave us the gift of marriage.
When sin marred that image
you healed our brokenness,
giving your Son to die for us.
Therefore we raise our voices,
with all who have served you in every age,
to proclaim the glory of your name:

Prayer after Communion

This is a presidential text but it also lends itself to be said together by all.

Gracious God,
may N and N, who have been bound together
in these holy mysteries,
become one in body and soul.
May they live in faithfulness and peace
and obtain those eternal joys
prepared for all who love you;
through your Son, Jesus Christ our Lord.

All **Amen.**

The Dismissal

The blessing comes, in this form, from *Patterns for Worship*.

The Lord bless you and keep you:

All **Amen.**

The Lord make his face to shine upon you,
and be gracious to you:

All **Amen.**

The Lord lift up his countenance upon you
and give you peace:

All **Amen.**

The Lord God almighty, Father, Son and Holy Spirit,
the holy and undivided Trinity,
guard you, save you,
and bring you to that heavenly city,
where he lives and reigns for ever and ever.

All **Amen.**

Numbers 6.24-26

Prayers at the Calling of the Banns

The legal requirement of reading banns is a pastoral opportunity. It is good to encourage couples to come to church to hear their names being read aloud, even better to hear themselves being prayed for by name, and even better again to be welcomed formally or informally by the congregation. One valuable encouragement to couples is to have their banns read not too far before their wedding day – say in the month before, so that as anticipation grows, so does an awareness of the role of the Church. However, great care must be taken not to forget to call the banns and to check that the original information provided is still valid at the time of calling. It is wise to leave a Sunday or two in which to correct any mishaps.

Note 2 states that the banns are to be published in the church on three Sundays at the time of Divine Service by the officiant in the form set out in *The Book of Common Prayer* or in the following form. This does not mean the three Sundays have to be consecutive, so couples stand a good chance of arranging dates when they can be present.

I publish the banns of marriage between *NN* of ... and *NN* of
...This is the *first (second) (third)* time of asking. If any of you
know any reason in law why they may not marry each other
you are to declare it.

We pray for these couples *(or N and N)* as they prepare for
their wedding(s).

The Supplementary Texts provide two prayers for use when there
is more than one couple whose banns are being read or one
couple only, using their own names. This will be new to some
parishes but many have already become used to this spiritual
approach to a legal requirement.

Lord,
the source of all true love,
we pray for *these couples.*
Grant to them
joy of heart,
seriousness of mind,
and reverence of spirit,
that as they enter into the oneness of marriage
they may be strengthened and guided by you,
through Jesus Christ our Lord.
Amen.

Lord of love,
we pray for *N* and *N.*
Be with them in all their preparations
and on their wedding day.
Give them your love in their hearts
throughout their married life together,
through Jesus Christ our Lord.
Amen.

Members of the congregation can be encouraged to come
forward to offer this prayer. It can be really moving for a couple
to see a worshipping community at prayer for them and their
marriage.

3 Thanksgiving for Marriage

This is a new service to the Church, in its formal provision at least. It is a good example of the power of pastoral need, as clergy have often been asked to provide such liturgical moments, yet without formal resourcing by the Church. Most clergy will be able to describe several very different circumstances when couples have come forward asking for some kind of thanksgiving or renewal without quite knowing themselves what they are asking for. The response has had to be flexible and innovative. I can recall a variety of examples: I have been asked for a blessing at the end of a weekday service, for a thanksgiving at a silver wedding anniversary party, and for a service of dedication to God after many years in a second marriage. The idea of a more general celebration was also rejected by my congregation. There are so many issues involved in this area that the Church has needed a flexible service to be able to respond creatively to such requests.

Once I was in church when the preacher extolled the virtues of marriage, upsetting all those in the congregation who, for a variety of reasons, had suffered marriage breakdown. The preacher's marriage broke down soon after. Our churches are full of folk who have memories of marriage that are both 'for better' and 'for worse' and any enthusiasm to use this new service must take this into serious consideration.

Just as every marriage is different, so are the views of married couples when it comes to the renewal of marriage vows. Some value an annual celebration, some choose to mark particular anniversaries with an act of recommitment and some like to keep the memory of their once and for all event pure in their memory by never renewing what is made for ever. I can find all these responses in my own congregation and also much tension about renewing what for some is lost for ever. Great sensitivity is required when planning a thanksgiving for marriage. This new service is designed to apply to the case of the individual couple and the more general celebration for a larger number of couples.

The prefatory Note itself states that the outline service is designed for a number of different occasions. It may be used

- on occasions when a number of couples reaffirm their vows together;
- to celebrate an anniversary;
- after a time of separation or difficulty in marriage;
- either at home or in church;
- combined with another service, such as the Holy Communion.

Couples who have come to faith years after being married in a civil ceremony also sometimes ask for such a service rather than the Service of Prayer and Dedication after a Civil Marriage.

For each occasion, suitable prayers and other words should be chosen, with the couple (if appropriate), from the suggested resources or elsewhere. Informality and extempore prayer are encouraged, especially in more informal settings.

The suggested service owes a lot to the ASB and incorporates some of the best aspects of the new *Common Worship* Marriage Service. The key to using this service is in the rubrics which often imply that a choice is to be made in accordance with the pastoral context. Again, imaginative use of the church building may be required, especially if the desire is to avoid a mock-up of a past wedding. Individual parts of this service can be used in a service of Holy Communion.

One obvious suggestion is to hold such a thanksgiving during a Sunday morning service. The reading of the account of the wedding at Cana in Galilee from John's Gospel provides a useful focus for such a service. Couples married during the previous year can be invited, as can couples from the coming year, and the whole congregation can join in an affirmation of Christian marriage whether they are married themselves or not. It may be necessary to hold such a service bi-annually if weddings are few in number.

A pastoral responsibility here is to be aware of those who, because of difficulties in their own marriage relationship, or because of a previous marriage that has ended, may find such an act of thanksgiving painful. It is also important to consider the feelings of single people before embarking upon a grand celebration of marriage.

Thanksgiving for Marriage: An Outline Order

Introduction

Welcome and Introduction

Prayer of Preparation

Preface

Readings

Psalms, Songs or Hymns

Sermon

Renewal of Vows

The couple(s) are invited to renew their marriage vows in a suitable form;

A ring or rings may be blessed,

Prayers are offered including prayers of thanksgiving and blessing.

The structure of the service

Introduction

The Welcome

> *The minister welcomes the people, introduces the service*
> *informally, and invites those present to pray.*

This rubric is more specific than the similar one in the same place
in the Marriage Service itself. The minister invites those present to
pray, setting the tone and nature of this pastoral celebration. The
comments in Chapter 2 about use of the Grace also apply here.

> The grace of our Lord Jesus Christ,
> the love of God,
> and the fellowship of the Holy Spirit
> be with you
> *All* **and also with you.**

> *This sentence may be used*
> God is love, and those who live in love live in God
> and God lives in them.
>
> *1 John 4.16*

Prayer of Preparation
This prayer is taken from the ASB and acts as an opening collect,
becoming more relevant in its use here, where the phrase
'continue in your love until their lives' end' has more pertinence.

> God our Father
> you have taught us through your Son
> that love is the fulfilling of the law:
> grant to your servants N and N
> that, loving one another,
> they may continue in your love until their lives' end;
> through Jesus Christ our Lord.
> *All* **Amen.**

Preface

This Preface is adapted from the Alternative Preface (see the Supplementary Texts) in the main Marriage Service provision. Two parts are optional: firstly, 'to ask forgiveness for all that has been amiss', which should be used only when a couple are celebrating their reconciliation; and secondly, 'it is given as the foundation of family life . . .' is optional to allow for the possibility of a childless marriage. The rubric that follows the Preface asks specifically for constructive silence and should be introduced as an important moment of reflection.

We have come together in the presence of God
to give thanks [*with N and N*] for [. . . *years of*] married life,
[to ask his forgiveness for all that has been amiss,]
to rejoice together and to ask for God's blessing.
As our Lord Jesus Christ was himself a guest
at the wedding in Cana of Galilee,
so through his Spirit he is with us now.
Marriage is a gift of God in creation
and a means of his grace;
it is given that a husband and wife
may comfort and help each other,
living faithfully together
in times of need as well as in plenty,
in sadness and in joy, in sickness and in health;
it is given that with delight and tenderness
they may know each other in love
[it is given as the foundation of family life
in which children may be born and nurtured
in accordance with God's will, to his praise and glory].
In marriage a couple belong together
and live life in the community;
it is a way of life created and hallowed by God,
that all should honour.
Therefore we pray with them
that, strengthened and guided by God,
they may continue to fulfil his purpose for their life together.

Silence is kept for reflection on the years that have passed, and on shared experiences, good and bad.

Readings and Sermon

> *One or more passages of Holy Scripture are read. Psalms or hymns may follow the readings. Other songs and readings may be used. A sermon may be preached.*

Renewal of Vows

> *The minister says to the couple(s)*
>
> I invite you now to recall the vows that you made at your wedding.
>
> *Husband and wife face each other and hold hands.*
>
> *The husband says*
>
> I, N, took you, N, to be my wife;
> *The wife says*
> I, N, took you, N, to be my husband;
> *The couple say together*
> to have and to hold from that day forward,
> for better, for worse, for richer, for poorer,
> in sickness and in health, to love and to cherish,
> till death us do part, according to God's holy law,
> and this was our solemn vow.
> Today, in the presence of our family and friends,
> we affirm our continuing commitment to this vow.
>
> *The minister says to the congregation*
>
> Will you, the family and friends of N and N
> continue to support and uphold them
> in their marriage now and in the years to come?
> *All* **We will.**

If the celebration involves many couples, it may be necessary for them to stand in their places, facing each other and perhaps holding hands, or for them all to simply move out into the main aisle of the church. The key word in the introduction is *recall*, rather than *renew*, as in the title of this section. Some couples feel strongly that they cannot renew that which was made once and for ever, so the words read by the minister make clear that what is happening is a recollection, not a repetition, of a past event.

The Rings

It is assumed here that this prayer can be used for different purposes. I well remember one of my first marriage couples returning from honeymoon in great distress, because the new husband had lost his wedding ring while swimming (that was his excuse anyway). This inauspicious start was soon rectified by the purchase and gift of another ring and the couple came to church for a short act of ring blessing. This prayer could have been used on just such an occasion.

If a new ring or new rings are to be blessed, this prayer may be used

Heavenly Father, source of everlasting love,
revealed to us in Jesus Christ
and poured into our hearts through your Holy Spirit;
that love which many waters cannot quench,
    neither the floods drown;
that love which is patient and kind, enduring all things
    without end;
by your blessing,
let *these rings* be to N and N
symbols to remind them of the covenant made on their
    wedding day,
through your grace in the love of your Son
and in the power of your Spirit.
All **Amen.**

If a ring (or rings) are to be given these words are used

I give you this ring
as a sign of our marriage.
With my body I honour you,
all that I am I give to you,
and all that I have I share with you,
within the love of God,
Father, Son and Holy Spirit.

Or, if not, each may touch the wedding ring(s) with the words

I gave you this ring
as a sign of our marriage.
With my body I honour you,
all that I am I give to you,
all that I have I share with you,
within the love of God,
Father, Son and Holy Spirit.

Prayers

This section includes various elements that perform different tasks. The first is an adapted prayer for nuptial blessing.

God the Father, God the Son, God the Holy Spirit,
bless, preserve and keep you;
the Lord mercifully grant the riches of his grace
that you may please him both in body and soul,
and, living together in faith and love,
may receive the blessings of eternal life.

All **Amen.**

Next follow the versicles and responses from the ASB, which serve as a useful response to the nuptial blessing.

Blessed are you, heavenly Father.
All **You give joy to husband and wife.**

Blessed are you, Lord Jesus Christ.
All **You have brought new life to mankind.**

Blessed are you, Holy Spirit of God.
All **You bring us together in love.**

Blessed be Father, Son and Holy Spirit.
All **One God, to be praised for ever. Amen.**

The longer and greater prayer of thanksgiving is, to a large extent, the dramatic climax of this service. Praying over a couple, perhaps with hands or arms extended, is a powerful sign of praise and thanksgiving. In this prayer the minister is

- praising almighty God;

- recalling the covenant of grace through the Holy Spirit;

- acknowledging the existing and continuing marriage relationship;

- recognizing the presence of Christ;

- calling for their lives to be a witness in a troubled world;

- asking for continued growth together;

- blessing their home;

- blessing their children (omitted if necessary);

- looking forward to our heavenly relationship with God.

Almighty God, our heavenly Father,
we lift up our hearts to you
through Jesus Christ our Lord.
Through him you have made a covenant of grace with your
     people
by the outpouring of your Holy Spirit.

We praise you for the gift of marriage
in which the love of husband and wife is brought together
and reflects your plan of love for the world.

We thank you today for N and N,
and for leading them to each other
in friendship and love, commitment and trust,
and for bringing them here for the blessing of their marriage.

Living God,
by the presence of your Holy Spirit,
may they know the risen Christ to be with them now,
as they celebrate this covenant together.
May their lives be a witness to your saving love
in this troubled world.

As you pour out your love,
may they grow together in your sight,
and each be to the other
a companion in joy, a comfort in sorrow and a strength in
    need.

As you blessed the earthly home at Nazareth
with the presence of your Son,
may their home be a place of security and peace.
[Bless this couple with the gift and care of children,
that they may grow up to know and love you in your Son.]
And bring us all at the last
to that great marriage banquet of your Son
in our home in heaven,
with all your saints and angels,
in the glory of your presence,
and for ever praise you through Jesus Christ our Lord.

All **Amen.**

The Lord's Prayer follows here.

The Dismissal

Here the couple may pray together. This is not easy to do aloud
with two voices and may work better in a smaller, more private
celebration. Another way of using this prayer is for each partner
to say alternate sentences, both joining in the final Amen. It is
easier to say this in unison at a larger celebration.

Heavenly Father,
we offer you our souls and bodies,
our thoughts and words and deeds,
our love for one another.
Unite our wills in your will,
that we may grow together
in love and peace
all the days of our life;
through Jesus Christ our Lord.

All **Amen.**

The final Trinitarian blessing recalls the Marriage Service itself.

God the Holy Trinity make you strong in faith and love,
defend you on every side, and guide you in truth and peace;
and the blessing of God almighty,
the Father, the Son and the Holy Spirit,
be among you and remain with you always.
Amen.

This new service will prove useful to the Church for a variety of pastoral reasons. It should be seen both as a whole and as a service with component parts that can be used independently for specific pastoral opportunities.

4 Resources in marriage liturgy

The purpose of this chapter is to unpack some of the resources available through the provision of the new service. Some ministers may like to produce their own adapted summaries of the available readings, prayers and hymns so that couples can make more informed choices.

Provision within *Common Worship*

Readings and Psalms

The following biblical references come from the Readings and Psalms in the Supplementary Texts for use with the *Common Worship* Marriage Service. The brief notes will help the minister describe the passage to the couple. Assuming a copy of the Marriage Service is given to each couple, an additional and similar printed summary can help the couple in their choices by enabling them to take it away and look up the references in their own time. Key passages and short summaries describe the content of each reference. It is worth checking whether a couple are familiar with how to look up a biblical reference, as otherwise the exercise is counter-productive.

The full texts are printed in *Pastoral Services* but clergy may wish to produce a simple 'home-grown' booklet with the readings printed in full.

Old Testament and Apocrypha

Genesis 1.26-28	*God created humankind, male and female; God blessed them and gave them dominion over every living thing that moves upon the earth.*
Song of Solomon 2.10-13; 8.6-7	*Arise, my love, my fair one, and come away. Love is as strong as death.*
Tobit 8.4-8	*On their wedding night Tobias and Sarah praise God and pray for their safety so that they may grow old together.*
Jeremiah 31.31-34	*A new covenant, God's law, written in our hearts, so we shall be his people.*

Epistles

Romans 7.1-2, 9-18	*Paul, using marriage as an analogy for the Christian life, says that according to the law, a person whose previous married partner has died is no longer bound by that marriage. The second part (9-18) calls sin the enemy and 'the flesh' refers to 'fallen' human nature.*
Romans 8.31-35, 37-39	*If God is for us, who is against us? An expression of the Christian's confidence in God.*
Romans 12.1, 2, 9-13	*Present your bodies as a living sacrifice, be transformed to discern the will of God. This majestic passage continues at v. 9 with examples of the consecrated life and may be a useful alternative to 1 Corinthians 13.*

Romans 15.1-3, 5-7, 13	*Paul describes people living in harmony, in accordance with Christ Jesus, with all joy and peace in believing.*
1 Corinthians 13.1-13	*Love, the greatest gift and way.*
Ephesians 3.14-21	*To know the love of Christ is to be rooted and grounded in love. God is the author of all family relationships.*
Ephesians 4.1-6	*Patience, bearing with one another in love; an appeal to maintain unity through the one God and Father of all.*
Ephesians 5.21-33	*Be subject to one another out of reverence for Christ. This description of the Christian household is about mutual self-giving, mirroring Jesus' love for his people.*
Philippians 4.4-9	*Rejoice in the Lord always; again I will say, Rejoice! An exhortation for personal growth that places all hope in the God of peace.*
Colossians 3.12-17	*The virtues of the Christian life grow from the new relationship with Jesus as chosen ones are clothed with a new nature. Do everything as if Jesus were doing it.*
1 John 3.18-24	*God, who knows everything, judges us by the abiding relationship of love to others, rather than by our passing moods. Love is evidence of God's Spirit and presence.*

| 1 John 4.7-12 | *Beloved, let us love another, because love is from God. To love one another is to have God in us, which influences our daily lives.* |

Gospel

Matthew 5.1-10	*The Beatitudes from the Sermon on the Mount, the keynote of the new age, proclaiming God's blessing upon all who live under his rule.*
Matthew 7.21, 24-29	*Firm foundations are needed for a long-lasting relationship.*
Mark 10.6-9, 13-16	*Jesus' teaching on marriage echoes God's creation purpose. From this comes the gift of children. We enter the Kingdom of God only 'as a child'.*
John 2.1-11	*At a village wedding at Cana in Galilee Jesus brings about a wonderful transformation, turning water into wine.*
John 15.1-8	*Growth and a fruitful life depend on being one with Christ, the 'true vine'.*
John 15.9-17	*The passage continues, showing that the Christian life is a relationship of love. This is my commandment, that you love one another as I have loved you.*

Psalms

| Psalm 67 | *May God be gracious to us and bless us.* |
| Psalm 121 | *I lift up my eyes to the hills. A psalm of blessing as we journey through life.* |

Psalm 127

A safe home and a large family are the Lord's gift. Anxiety has no place in the life of the faithful.

Psalm 128

May you see your children's children. A large and prosperous family is a reward for devotion to the Lord.

Additional Prayers and Collects

The Supplementary Texts provide a wealth of material for selection. Couples will need some guidance as to how to make an informed choice and what is practical in the time available. The headings in the list of categories for prayer at a marriage service help couples to make this choice. If they realize how they may pray – with Thanksgiving; for Spiritual Growth; in Faithfulness, Joy, Love, for Forgiveness and Healing; and for others – they will soon be able to find prayers that speak for them. Extempore prayer is also permissible. This summary assumes that couples will be given a copy of the Marriage Service and then locally produced material to support the making of choices.

Longer Prayers and Litanies

1. A form of intercession, with a congregational response after a short bidding. The theme is growth and the harvest of the Spirit.

2. A prayer for all people, with congregational response. The theme is a broken world strengthened by holy relationships.

3. A more traditional and complex style of wording that acknowledges the challenges of married life.

4. An outpouring of praise that is also available in the service of Thanksgiving for Marriage. There is no congregational response.

Thanksgiving

5 For the sharing of love. The treasures of the kingdom are opened.

6 A prayer that shares blessing with all those present and with the couple on their wedding day.

Spiritual Growth

7 A prayer for the home, recalling Jesus' earthly home in Nazareth.

8 A prayer from *The Alternative Service Book 1980* seeking the gift of the Holy Spirit.

9 A prayer for the grace to live well, seeking one another's welfare, bearing one another's burdens and sharing joy.

10 A prayer that describes discipleship with all its gifts, but also all its challenges, and does not shirk the reality of the cost of following Christ in marriage.

11 Using the story of the wedding at Cana in Galilee as a theme, this prayer seeks a glimpse of eternal love.

12 A prayer for the gift of love, acknowledging that without God we cannot please him and asking God to send the Holy Spirit.

13 A prayer for marriage to be a sign to the world.

Faithfulness, Joy, Love, Forgiveness and Healing

14 A prayer that explicitly mentions the gift of sexual love as from God for the sharing of creation.

15 A pastoral prayer that can be used where there is division or sadness in a family. The specific intention is for the healing of memory.

16 A prayer evoking the laughter and pleasure of marriage, ending with an intention for the celebration of many wedding anniversaries.

17 A prayer for grace and delight that lends itself to be used at a wedding rehearsal.

18 A clear prayer for faithfulness.

19 Another prayer for faithfulness that mentions the solemn promises of marriage.

20 Another prayer for faithfulness that can also be used in preparation for marriage.

21 This prayer for faithfulness and peace may also be used as an opening prayer at the wedding reception.

22 This prayer from *The Alternative Service Book 1980* recalls the popular prayer of St Richard of Chichester and speaks of following Christ daily.

Children, other Family Members and Friends

23 This prayer has been a popular choice for the gift of children and a safe home.

24 A prayer for children and family that mentions the couple by name.

25 An important prayer that can be used where there is an existing family or children who will be affected by the new marriage relationship.

26 This prayer, which focuses on the families of the couple, could also be used at a wedding reception.

27 A final prayer for the support of friends which could be said by a friend at the service or later.

Canticles

Four canticles are provided for use by the minister, couple or congregation. Imaginative use can be made of these, such as the reading of alternate verses by different speakers (perhaps the couple themselves) or reading over meditative music. The suggested canticles are:

1 A Song of Solomon (Song of Solomon 6–8).

2 A Song of the Bride (Isaiah 61.10-11; 62.1-3).

3 Magnificat (The Song of Mary) (Luke 1.46-55).

4 A Song of the Lamb (Revelation 19.16, 56, 66-7, 96).

Hymns and Music

The Marriage Service in *Common Worship* contains no specific reference to hymns or music. However, the minister should help couples make good choices as music plays such an important part in weddings.

In all cases, early involvement of the organist/choir leader/director of music is essential. Those with professional expertise or longstanding, gifted experience are to be seen as key people in the successful celebration of a wedding. Ministers will be used to working closely with their music leaders and will be able to help couples make choices from what is available, possible, realistic and appropriate.

Processional and Recessional Music

Recently a bride gave me a CD that contains examples of processional and recessional music. This has transformed my wedding interviews as I am able to appear trendy by playing excerpts of appropriate music via remote control. The choice has become more informed and I am saved the embarrassment of trying to hum examples of Handel or Mendelssohn ('Wedding Bells: All the music you need for your special day'; Marks and Spencer CA 01295 CIFA – 37002516. T27 0600/4943).

Better still is when the couple find occasion to meet with the organist to hear real examples in church of music for their entering and leaving.

Popular choices might be:

Arrival of the Queen of Sheba – *Handel*

Bridal March from *Lohengrin* – *Wagner*

Crown Imperial March – *Walton*

Grand March from *Aida* – *Verdi*

Overture to the Music for the Royal Fireworks – *Handel*

Trumpet Voluntary – *Jeremiah Clarke*

Trumpet Tune and Air – *Purcell*

Hornpipe in F from the Water Music – *Handel*

Toccata (Symphony No.5) – *Widor*

Wedding March – *Mendelssohn*

Ode to Joy – *Beethoven*

The provision of music or singing during the Signing of the Registers has already been discussed but, whatever the form, this will always benefit from an introduction by the minister.

Hymns and Songs

The choice of hymnody at weddings has always been somewhat predictable. The classic, 'I remember that one from school', will perhaps never leave us. The task of the minister here is not to remove responsibility for hymn choice, nor to limit choice restrictively, but to ensure that the chosen selection fits together and that the right hymn is sung at the right place and at the right time in each service.

Many parishes have found it helpful to compile a list of suggested hymns, including the numbers, from their chosen hymnbook(s) and perhaps divide the subject matter into groups such as 'Hymns of Praise, Hymns of Love, Hymns of Hope' and so on. Good practice suggests that hymns should be well-known, not too long and used with the tunes (if there are alternatives) that the couple prefer. A list of suggested hymns and songs is provided here as a starting point for discussion. The world of hymnody and songs is constantly changing and this list is not meant to be exhaustive but to act as a prompt for parishes to compile their own list. For information on copyright, see Appendix 5.

All creatures of our God and King

All heaven declares

All people that on earth do dwell

All things bright and beautiful

Alleluia, sing to Jesus

Amazing grace

At the name of Jesus every knee shall bow

Be still, for the presence of the Lord

Bind us together

Blessed assurance, Jesus is mine

Blest be the tie that binds

Christ is made the sure foundation

Come down, O love divine

Come on and celebrate

Crown him with many crowns

Dear Lord and Father of mankind

Father, hear the prayer we offer

From heaven you came, helpless babe (The Servant King)

Give thanks with a grateful heart

Great is the Lord and most worthy of praise

Great is thy faithfulness

Guide me, O thou great Redeemer

Give me joy in my heart

Here we are, gathered together as a family

I cannot tell why he whom angels worship

Immortal, invisible, God only wise

Jesus is Lord! Creation's voice proclaims it

Jesus put this song into our hearts

Jesus, stand among us at the meeting of our lives

Jesus, the Lord of love and life

Lead us, heavenly Father

Let all the world in every corner sing

Let there be love shared among us

Lord Jesus Christ, invited guest and saviour

Lord Jesus Christ, you have come to us

Lord of all hopefulness

Lord, for the years your love has kept and guided

Lord, the light of your love is shining (Shine, Jesus, shine)

Love divine, all loves excelling

Make me a channel of your peace

May the fragrance of Jesus fill this place

Morning has broken

New every morning is the love

Now thank we all our God

O for a heart to praise my God

O for a thousand tongues to sing

O God beyond all praising, we worship you today

O Jesus, I have promised

O Lord my God, when I in awesome wonder

O Lord, your tenderness

O worship the King

Praise, my soul, the King of heaven

Praise to the Lord, the Almighty, the king of creation

Rejoice! rejoice

Rejoice, the Lord is King

Seek ye first the kingdom of God

Shine, Jesus, shine

Such love

Tell out, my soul

The King of love my shepherd is

The Lord's my shepherd

Thine be the glory

This is the day

To God be the glory!

You are the vine, we are the branches

You shall go out with joy

Other marriage liturgy available to the Church

This book is about the new *Common Worship* Marriage Service but it must take note of the other authorized liturgies that are available for clergy and couples to choose.

Many couples come forward asking for the old service, perhaps not knowing for what they are really asking. Mostly this is because of family prompting or hesitation about a particular liturgical style or, most frequently, a desire to have a traditional service, often symbolized by which version of the Lord's Prayer is used. It is important that couples know that there are choices available to them but that most weddings are 'traditional' in flavour. The real decision is about what style of language is preferred by the couple and how much choice they would like in the various components of their service.

The Book of Common Prayer

The Book of Common Prayer remains unaffected by the process of liturgical change. All the new services, as with the ASB, are 'alternative' to this historic provision which is still in popular use today. The Prayer Book is part of our Anglican heritage and still has liturgical and theological importance for the Church. The *Common Worship* process has sought to value the Prayer Book tradition and to set that alongside the modern, so that both may be seen as legitimate parts of the Church of England's liturgical experience.

Characteristics of the Prayer Book service (where it differs significantly from other texts) may be summarized as follows:

- dramatic language with powerful imagery;
- vocabulary not in common use today ('men's carnal lusts' . . . 'brute beasts' . . . 'godly matrons' etc.);
- the woman must 'obey';
- the use of only one ring;
- a summary of the duties of man and wife.

Most clergy will make allowances in a service to accommodate modern expressions of the marriage commitment (such as the exchange of rings or the woman choosing not to promise to obey) but it is important that couples are enabled to choose this service if they wish to do so. The essence in all this is that informed choices are good choices and should be respected.

Alternative Services, First Series

The Series 1 Solemnization of Matrimony (1966) finds its root in the proposed Prayer Book of 1928. It is a popular version of *The Book of Common Prayer* service and is authorized until 2005. My wife and I were married using this service. The main characteristics of this service are as follows:

- traditional but more familiar liturgical language;

- an option on whether the woman should choose to 'obey';

- the option to have identical vows;

- still the possibility of one ring only being given.

Once again, most clergy have adapted this service to include the exchange of rings and to be more flexible on the use of prayers. For those who look for a service using 'thee' and 'thy' rather than 'you' and 'your' this remains a popular choice.

An Order of Marriage for Christians from Different Churches

The Joint Liturgical Group of Great Britain has produced a new service to be used when the marriage partners are from different denominations.

It seeks to bring together various understandings of marriage: the Western emphasis on consent in which a couple's promise is recognized and supported; the Jewish and Eastern emphasis that sees marriage as a gift to both couple and community; the civic tradition that gives public recognition of the marriage.

The service is designed to meet the current legal requirements for marriage while allowing flexibility: it can be adapted to meet individual needs and preferences. This service has been authorized for use by the Church of England but will not be printed in the new *Common Worship* material.

The service is available in a useful handbook that gives good advice, not only about the liturgical situation, but also the legal constraints involved and the pastoral issues of such a marriage. The handbook is:

> *An Order of Marriage For Christians from Different Churches*, The Joint Liturgical Group of Great Britain, Canterbury Press, Norwich. ISBN 1-85311-309-3, £3.99.

Even if this service is more important as a triumph of ecumenism than the kind of service that will be used by a great number of couples, it does contain useful liturgical ideas. An Affirmation by Families and Congregation is included and an explicit Invocation of the Holy Spirit. There is a Prayer for Grace and the opportunity for genuine cooperation between ministers of the differing traditions. To me, the most interesting aspect is the Presentation of Gift(s) from the Churches, which may be accompanied by words of support and good wishes. The mind boggles as to where this will take us if it should be picked up in all weddings with many and various folk presenting gifts, but here is a real opportunity for evangelism in all our different traditions and circumstances.

Symbolic gifts may be presented to the couple by representatives of the church communities from which the couple come. As the gifts are given, the affirmation, support and good wishes of the churches for the couple may be voiced.

For example, a Bible may be presented with these words:

> Let the message of Christ, in all its richness, find a home
>   with you:
> Teach each other and advise each other in all wisdom.
>
> (Colossians 3.16)

> *or*

> . . . church wishes you well, and offers you this . . .
> for a gift on your wedding day.

Outline of the Rite

An asterisk (*) indicates optional elements that may be included where appropriate.

Hymns may be introduced at any appropriate point.

Preparation and Introduction

Welcome

Greeting

Opening Prayer

Statement of Marriage

Legal Declarations

Declaration of Intent

*Affirmation by Families and Congregation

Prayer of Invocation

Ministry of the Word

Readings from Scripture

Sermon

Hymn

The Marriage

Prayer for Grace

The Marriage Vows (Exchange of Consent)

The Giving of the Rings(s)

The Prayer of Blessing

The Announcement of Marriage

[The Prayer of Blessing – alternative position]

*Presentation of Gift(s) from the Churches

Signing of Registers

Hymn

After the Marriage

Prayers

The Lord's Prayer

*The Peace
*Holy Communion
Dismissal of the Congregation
[Signing of Registers – alternative position]

An Order for Prayer and Dedication after a Civil Marriage

This service will be familiar to many, having been commended by the House of Bishops in 1985. It has become a flexible tool to meet people in their pastoral need without compromising the traditional position of the Church on re-marriage. This service is reproduced in the format of *Common Worship* in the *Pastoral Services* book. Canon B 4 still applies and it is important to meet any bishop's guidelines that may be in force in a given diocese. Particular reference should be made to the notes for this service which provide guidance on its use.

Symbolism in Marriage Liturgy

Any marriage service is rich in symbolism. Special clothing, the exchange of rings, perhaps the celebration of the Eucharist, all contribute to support the words of the liturgy. Actions do often speak louder than words. Secular symbols also find their way into weddings – such as chimney sweeps for good luck. Any symbol must not detract from the service itself but serve as a pastorally appropriate picture of what is taking place. Ministers are being asked for such symbols with increasing frequency so an awareness of typical requests and their meaning may be helpful. These symbols do not form part of the textual provision of the *Common Worship* Marriage Service – other than the symbol of rings, of course. A greater description of these symbols may be found in *To Join Together* by Kenneth Stevenson (for details see Note 6, p. 24).

1. Exchange of Rings

The ring is perhaps the most popular symbol of marriage and couples attach a great deal of importance to the exchange. The ring is a sign of unending love and faithfulness and a reminder of promises made. According to folklore, a wedding ring is worn on the fourth finger of the left hand to restrain the forces of evil that might lead a person astray as there is a direct link between that finger and the heart. It is important that couples are not encouraged to be superstitious about their rings. Obviously it is important to wear the ring, but some forms of work require the removal of all jewellery and it may be necessary to remove rings before medical treatment.

2. Precious coins

This is an old custom from Lincolnshire and Ireland. A coin is given after the exchange of rings; today this might be adapted into personal wedding gifts.

3. Canopy

Many will associate the use of a canopy with Jewish tradition but it is also found in the Lutheran churches, where a canopy, held with four poles, is placed over the couple during the service, symbolizing God's presence covering the couple. The canopy may be held by friends or family and may be decorated with flowers or embroidery.

4. Crowning

This Eastern Orthodox tradition suggests that the couple are being treated as royalty for the day or crowned with glory. Crowns can be made from metal or flowers and are held by attendants above the heads of the bride and groom to symbolize the special grace God gives in marriage.

5. Anointing

Marriage is clearly a vocation and so anointing with oil is a sign of the sealing of God's call. Some parishes anoint at the start of marriage preparation. The laying on of hands with prayer could also accompany this symbol, or be used on its own as a powerful sign of God's activity.

6. Binding

Spain has the ancient custom of binding a couple together with some form of rope. This could send confusing signals in our culture and so it may be better to make more of the commonly accepted act of binding with the stole of a priest. This usually takes place in the sight of the couple only but could be made more dramatic and meaningful if seen more clearly by the whole congregation.

7. Candles

Candles have become fashionable. The new couple will more than likely decorate their house with candles. Whilst it is important not to have 'candles with everything', there is a popular ceremony originating in America which has powerful symbolism. The two outer candles of a triple-stemmed candelabra are lit, the candles could even be the baptismal candles of the couple. These candles represent their lives at the moment, distinct and individual. The couple take each candle, together light the central candle and then extinguish their individual candles. This central candle represents their union; like a flame, it cannot be divided but can light other flames. This candle then becomes their wedding candle and can be lit on their wedding anniversary each year.

Signs and symbols in the new service

Whether such symbols are incorporated into the service or not, it is useful to be able to describe the powerful symbolism of any marriage service. This can be helpful at the time of preparation and rehearsal. For example, it can be very productive to spend time with couples unpacking the symbolism of the service itself. One such aspect is the joining of hands. The importance of this action is often missed. The vows are made whilst bride and groom hold each other's hand, the person making the vow holding the right hand of the other. This is action speaking with words, for just as the marriage is made by the spoken vow, so it is also made by the physical touch, symbolizing together the marriage of body, mind and soul. Folk tradition tells of right hands being preferred to left hands for a number of superstitious reasons but the common custom of using the right hand to make contracts is the most likely origin for this. Likewise, the binding of the marriage at the Proclamation is a symbolic sealing of what has just taken place.

The rings are, of course, the most obvious symbol. Rings act as signs of the marriage, public statements of married life. The majority of couples now choose to wear rings, avoiding overtones of ownership when only the woman wears the one ring. Rings are important symbols, as shown by their inclusion in the new service of Thanksgiving for Marriage. New rings may be exchanged or original rings valued as continuing symbols of the marriage commitment. Once again, though, it is important not to be superstitious about such symbols: many clergy have had to encourage couples to choose a new ring when one has been lost, and then have it blessed again in a short liturgical act. Rings are symbols of the marriage and are not the marriage itself.

Another familiar symbol is confetti. Clear and fair information about its use is helpful but it is also good to be able to tell couples and congregations that confetti is meant to 'blow' the couple on their way, aided by the prayers of their supporters. It is not always easy for those who care for church grounds to see it in this way.

Signs and symbols are used throughout Christian liturgy to help us articulate the activity of God's love. In marriage, these symbols are well known in the community and can therefore be used by clergy and others to teach about marriage in its widest Christian meaning.

5 Marriage and the law

The work of the clergy is primarily spiritual and pastoral, and this applies as much to their task of preparing couples for marriage as to anything else.

Marriage, however, is an institution in society which requires a framework of law, and the clergy will not be efficient pastors of those who come to them in connection with marriage if they cannot provide clear and accurate information and advice about the legal aspects of the matter. Moreover, in conducting a wedding service, the officiating minister becomes in effect an officer of the law, which makes it doubly important that he or she has a sound working knowledge of the legalities involved.

Archbishop George Carey;
from the Foreword to *Anglican Marriage in England and Wales: A Guide to the Law for Clergy*

This extract makes plain that all ministers share a responsibility to understand the law regarding marriage. This chapter seeks to unpack some of the information needed for clergy as it relates directly to the liturgical celebration of a marriage. Clergy are often not fully conversant with all the legal requirements of each individual case and if good training is not given mistakes can happen. I had a visit recently from one couple seeking a wedding in our parish church as this was the bride's parental home. No longer resident in the parish, the bride then presented her fiancé, a young man from South Africa. My first answers to their difficult questions about qualification were important in terms of their pastoral needs. Although it probably did not help that I was in the middle of a family Sunday lunch at the time, we are making good progress!

An essential tool

The most important point of reference for ministers is the following vital document: *Anglican Marriage in England and Wales: A Guide to the Law for Clergy* (see Appendix 6 for

further details). The following summary is not meant in any way
to cut short the booklet but is an encouragement to clergy
(within this book about the new Marriage Service) to be fully
aware of the legal responsibilities of their office. Much of the
material is lifted directly from the booklet as it offers such good
advice. These examples reflect the most regularly needed
information about the law for clergy but are in most cases only
abbreviations of fuller advice and obligations. When celebrating
marriage, the Church must balance the privilege and the duty.

1. Introduction

The information provided in *A Guide to the Law for Clergy*
(henceforth called 'the purple booklet') is believed to be correct
as at 1 September 1999.

Services of Prayer and Dedication after a Civil Marriage do not
require any formal preliminaries or registration. As such they fall
within the field of liturgical law rather than marriage law and
may be subject to differing diocesan regulations.

2. The pastoral aspect

'Officiating clergy, local clergy and surrogates should all be
mindful of the image of the Church that a couple receives when
going through the preliminaries to marriage.'

3. Buildings available for Anglican marriage

Anglican marriage may be solemnized only in a parish church, a
parish centre of worship or in a chapel licensed for marriages by
the bishop. Generally, if there is in a request for a service in a
place that is a departure from the norm, the archdeacon, diocesan
registrar, or the Faculty Office should be consulted at an early
stage.

The Archbishop of Canterbury may grant a special licence for
Anglican marriage at any place in England or Wales but only in
extraordinary circumstances.

The provisions of the Marriage Act 1994, which allow premises
other than register offices to be approved for the solemnization of
marriages, apply to civil marriages only.

4. Factors governing the choice of location

The basic rule is that for any marriage in a parish church or parish centre of worship, one of the parties must live in the parish.

A person who lives in one parish, but habitually worships in the church of another parish, may marry in the latter church provided his/her name is on the church electoral roll of the latter parish.

5. The meaning of residence

This is a complicated issue that causes confusion for clergy and couples alike. Generally, the wording of the statute depends on the type of preliminary being used:

Banns:	'The parish in which one of the parties resides'
Common licence:	'– the parish . . . in which one of the persons to be married has had his or her usual place of residence for fifteen days immediately before the grant of the licence'
Superintendent Registrar's Certificate (SRC) (see item 8):	'– a registration district in which one of the persons to be married has resided . . . for the period of seven days immediately before the giving of the notice of marriage'.

So far as the common licence is concerned, a generous approach is suggested by the 'purple booklet', specifically for temporary absences. The residence requirement for banns does not have to be satisfied over a stated period, but simply at one instant in time, specifically at the time of banns application.

The 'purple booklet' admits that the law on residence is clearly susceptible of more than one interpretation. The view of the Faculty Office is that the word 'resides' for banns and SRC requires a physical presence and occupation of premises as a home. This need not be a permanent arrangement, but it must subsist at the relevant time. For common licences, the Faculty Office view is that 'usual place of residence' does not require a physical presence, but there must be throughout the fifteen-day period a place within the parish which can properly be regarded as the home of the person in question. In the final analysis, clergy will have to form their own conclusions on whether a genuine local residence has been shown, based on common sense and (in the case of common licences) directions and guidelines given by the bishop and/or vicar-general of each diocese.

6. The duty to marry parishioners

In England and Wales every resident of a parish is entitled to marry in his/her parish church if the usual preliminaries have been fulfilled.

The incumbent or priest-in-charge has the duty to solemnize the marriage of parishioners on request (or to provide an assistant curate to do so), and is guilty of neglect of duty if he/she refuses (for which disciplinary proceedings may be taken in the ecclesiastical courts).

The incumbent is nevertheless entitled to receive reasonable notice.

The incumbent is entitled to appoint the date and time of the marriage, provided he/she acts reasonably. The incumbent also decides whether to offer the services of the organist, choir and bell-ringers.

In England the form of the authorized service is a matter to be agreed between the incumbent and the parties, or for the bishop's decision if they disagree.

Arrangements for marriage are almost always made by mutual agreement rather than in reliance upon the letter of the law.

7. Banns

Banns must be published in the parish churches (or other licensed building) of both parties.

Banns are to be published on three Sundays preceding the marriage; there is no requirement for these to be consecutive Sundays.

Before publication, the incumbent is entitled to require seven days' written notice of the full names of the parties, their places of residence, and the length of time for which each one has resided at the place of residence stated. The incumbent does not have to ask for this notice.

Banns are to be published at a morning service even if that is not the main service of the day. Exceptions are if there is no morning service or if the morning service does not have a member of the clergy present. When a member of the clergy is officiating, they must call the banns. Where there is no clergy person present, provided the service is Morning or Evening Prayer and at the usual time, banns are published in that church, a lay person (normally an officiating reader) may read the banns. Forms of wording for banns are provided; they do not require the current marital status of the parties to be inserted.

Objections to banns should not be permitted to disrupt a service. Whether an objection appears to be well founded or not, the person publishing banns should state that the objection is noted, and that the objector should see him/her after the service to give particulars of the objection; he/she should then proceed with the service (or with the calling of any other banns). Allegations of legal impediments should be investigated before the marriage is due to take place if they are prima facie supported by evidence. Objections that do not amount to legal impediments cannot be entertained. The clergy should seek advice from the diocesan registrar on any objection.

For each building in which banns may be published, the parochial church council is required to supply a register book of banns in a prescribed form. The person publishing banns is to read from the book and 'not from loose papers'. After each publication the person publishing banns is to sign the book.

If banns are published in one church for marriage in another, it will be necessary for a certificate to be issued that banns have been published in the former church in accordance with the Marriage Act. The officiant must see this certificate before the marriage goes ahead.

A marriage after banns must be solemnized within three calendar months from the last publication.

The current Parochial Fees Order prescribes fees which are to be charged for the publication of banns and issue of a certificate. The fees should be paid when the parties apply for banns to be published.

8. Superintendent Registrar's Certificate (SRC)

The SRC procedure is rarely used for Anglican marriage, so reference should be made to the 'purple booklet'.

9. Common licence

Marriage by common licence may take place on the basis of one party's qualifying residence, without any action being necessary where the other party lives; as a preliminary it is quicker than banns.

The normal qualifying residence is that one party has had his/her usual place of residence, for fifteen days immediately before applying for the licence, in the parish or district where the marriage is to take place, or is on the church electoral roll of the parish.

A marriage that takes place in England or Wales according to the law as set out in the 'purple booklet' will be held valid (as to form) by the courts of England and Wales, whatever the nationality of the parties. There is a risk, however, that it will not be valid under the law of the foreign country concerned. The Church recognizes a responsibility to prevent, if possible, those whose marriages it solemnizes from falling into this situation.

Accordingly, it is strongly recommended that even if marriage after banns is legally possible, Anglican marriage should be by common licence if either party is a national of a country outside the Old Commonwealth (Canada, Australia, New Zealand and South Africa), the European Union and the United States. In many dioceses it is further recommended that applications should be made to the diocesan registry rather than to a surrogate, and that the applicant should obtain from the relevant embassy or consulate, and submit at the time of the application, a letter confirming that a marriage in this country is valid in the country in question.

Common licences are essentially an exercise of the episcopal power of dispensation, whereby the bishop dispenses with the requirement of banns. The bishop's judicial powers may be exercised by his vicar-general (normally the chancellor of the diocese), and the vicar-general in turn may delegate the hearing of licence applications to surrogates. Thus it happens that most applications are made to relatively local clergy who have been appointed 'surrogates for marriages'. One of the couple seeking to marry by common licence should appear (by appointment) before the surrogate or at the registry, bringing any documentation required. An application form is then completed, and the applicant is required to confirm on oath that the details are true and that no impediment is known. If satisfied, the surrogate 'grants the licence' (technically speaking) then and there; however, in practice all licence documents are issued from the diocesan registry. The officiating minister should insist upon seeing the sealed licence before solemnizing the marriage.

A marriage by common licence must be solemnized within three calendar months from the date of the affidavit.

10. Special licence

The Archbishop of Canterbury enjoys the unique right to grant a special licence for marriage at any convenient time or place in England or Wales. This jurisdiction is sparingly exercised, and good cause must always be shown why a more normal preliminary to Anglican marriage cannot be used.

The most common need for a special licence is the parties' desire to marry in a building not normally authorized for Anglican marriage or in a parish where they cannot satisfy the residence requirement. Even in the last case good cause must be shown, normally in the form of a real connection with the parish or the church in question: the special licence procedure is not intended to enable parties to choose a church building on purely aesthetic grounds.

The procedure set out on pages 28–30 of the 'purple booklet' must be followed in these cases and early contact made with the Faculty Office. The Office also publishes a number of leaflets on aspects of marriage preliminaries, including the Special Licence procedure. This information is also posted on the Faculty web site.

Applications may be lodged at any time up to eighteen months before the date of the marriage and early application is strongly advised, before other arrangements are confirmed. The licence itself is not issued until close to the date of the wedding and, in common with other Anglican preliminaries, is valid for three months.

11. Registrar-General's Licence
A Registrar-General's Licence cannot be issued for Anglican marriages.

12. Recognition of divorce and nullity decrees

The Church of England follows the law of the land as regards capacity to marry. The fact that the clergy may be free from any obligation to solemnize the marriage of a person whose marriage has been dissolved by a court in the United Kingdom does not alter the fact that such a person is, in law, free to marry. The Church will recognize the validity of such second marriages and clergy are legally free to solemnize them, even though the Convocation of Canterbury expressed the view in 1957 that the Church should not allow the use of the Marriage Service in such cases, and many clergy consequently decline to officiate.

Clergy should bear in mind that a marriage is dissolved only by a decree absolute of divorce. They should always ask to see the decree, bearing the court seal (which takes the form of a rubber stamp), and ensure that it is not merely a decree 'nisi'.

The Church will also recognize a declaration of nullity made by a court in the United Kingdom, that is, a declaration that there is no valid marriage in existence. A parish priest has the same obligation to marry a parishioner whose marriage has been annulled as would exist if the parishioner had never gone through a form of marriage. A decree of nullity is made only in decree absolute form; there is no decree 'nisi'.

The Church of England does not recognize nullity decrees made by Roman Catholic marriage tribunals within the UK.

13. Kindred and affinity

Marriage between a person and any of the following relatives is totally prohibited: parent, child, adopted child, grandparent, grandchild, sibling, aunt or uncle, niece or nephew.

Other restrictions apply, for which the 'purple booklet' should be consulted.

14. The marriage service

An Anglican marriage must take place between 8 a.m. and 6 p.m., unless a Special Licence has been granted for another time, usually only for urgent medical reason.

Anglican marriage must follow the authorized rites of the Church of England. The options are: the BCP (1662), Series 1 (based on the proposed 1928 Prayer Book) and, from Advent Sunday 2000, *Common Worship*: The Marriage Service.

Important advice is given regarding a celebration with deaf persons present.

15. Ministers officiating at marriages

The officiant at Anglican marriages should normally be a bishop or priest, and a deacon may officiate only with the consent of the incumbent or priest in charge. The rite, on such occasions, should be used without variation. A deacon should rarely, if ever, solemnize a marriage in the first year of ordination.

16. Objections at the marriage service

An objection at the marriage service cannot render ineffective a previously valid publication of banns, including the marriage of an under-age minor if the parent has failed to object.

If legal impediments are alleged, a clear prima facie case should be made if the minister is to delay the service, and where such a case is made (or if there is any doubt) the minister should seek advice from the diocesan registrar as soon as possible. Under the Prayer Book rubric, the objector is obliged to give security for the costs that the parties may sustain, both in dealing with his/her allegation and on account of the delay in marriage. He/she can either deposit the required sum forthwith, or undertake to pay it if his/her allegations are held to be unfounded or show no valid impediment. In the latter event, sureties of known financial standing may be required to guarantee his/her undertaking. Obviously it is extremely difficult for the clergy to assess such costs, and undesirable for a lengthy financial discussion to take place in the service. The objector's willingness in principle to bear costs, coupled with a prima facie case, should be enough to warrant a reference to the diocesan registrar.

Objections not covered by the above should not be allowed to delay the service. The minister should indicate politely that the objection is noted, but that he/she intends to proceed. Afterwards the facts may be reported to the registrar or the bishop if it seems appropriate. If the minister has indicated that he/she intends to proceed but the objector seems set to prevent him/her doing so, the objector should be dealt with in the same way as any other disturber of public worship.

All this is a good reason for ensuring that the minister always has sidespersons and others available to him/her to deal with any such situation.

17. Registration

Following an Anglican marriage, it is the duty of the officiating minister to register the marriage immediately in duplicate books supplied for the purpose.

Entries in marriage register books must contain all the details required by the printed form; the couple are required to provide these details on request.

An entry is not complete until signed by the minister; any error discovered before the minister signs may be corrected forthwith, so that the error and the correction are both legible. Corrections to entries after the minister has signed may be made (by a note in the margin of the register, without obliterating the original entry) within one month of the entry in question. The minister who made the entry must make and date the correction (in both register books) in the presence of the married couple, and all three must sign it. If the couple cannot attend when the correction is made, the churchwardens of the parish may act in their place.

So long as a minister has custody of a register book (original or duplicate), he/she is required to permit searches in the book at reasonable times, and to give a signed certificate of any entry. Fees for searches and certificates are prescribed by statutory instrument from time to time.

18. Fees for marriage

Where Anglican marriage takes place in a parish church in England, fees are payable in accordance with the current Parochial Fees Order made by the Church Commissioners.

A reminder

Once again, all ministers have a duty to understand these legal requirements and to apply the law in the context of their pastoral ministry.

Conclusion

The new Marriage Service has the fewest number of changes from the ASB out of any of the new services found in *Common Worship*. It is not a radical departure but neither is it a service the Church can afford to take for granted.

So many opinions are formed about the Church, and therefore also about our faith, in this very public act of worship. People remember the experience of their marriage in church for a lifetime.

The new service provides an opportunity for parishes to review their practice and make the most of their provision, confident that the new service will not adversely challenge their general practice to date.

In essence, the Church must place the same importance and enthusiasm upon each marriage service as do the couple themselves. After all, we do have the privilege of sharing in the miracle of turning water into wine.

Appendix 1

A suggestion for a PCC study on the new Marriage Service

With the introduction of *Common Worship*, it is important that church members are informed of the changes that are taking place in the content and pattern of regular services. There are many ways of doing this, but one opportunity might be to spend time at a PCC or ministry team meeting looking at the new service. The shape of such a discussion could be as follows, although it will need to be adapted to fit the local situation.

Aim:	To share the new *Common Worship* services with the PCC or ministry team in order to increase awareness; to encourage prayerful participation in the celebration of marriage and practical participation in the pastoral policy of the parish.
Beware:	Don't be sidetracked into discussion about policy on remarriage, cohabitation or other marriage related issues of the day.
	Do state that any discussion about marriage services will bring back happy memories for some and disappointment or hurt for others, so all must be sensitive to the feelings of those around them.
Preparation:	Think about how you might want to review your policy on marriage in the light of the new resources.
	Provide copies of the new text.
Introduction:	Read the Pastoral Introduction.
Reflection:	Brief description of what the pastoral approach to wedding couples currently is in the parish. If appropriate, ask for contributions about experiences of weddings attended.

Changes: Outline the major changes in the new service:

> Structure
> Declaration by the people
> Greater resources
> The place of the registration
> Prayers at the Calling of Banns
> Thanksgiving for Marriage service

Discussion: How will the new service help challenge or develop the pastoral policy of the parish?

How can the parish provide clear information for couples?

Can the church develop its marriage preparation, perhaps involving more people from the congregation?

Scripture: Read and reflect upon one of the marriage readings, for example
John 2.1-11, the Marriage at Cana.

Prayer: Conclude with open prayer or with the prayer as set in the
Gathering:
God of wonder and of joy . . .

Appendix 2
Help with marriage issues

There are a range of agencies and voluntary organizations that offer help with issues around marriage. The following contact points are offered here for reference.

Anglican Marriage Encounter

Anglican Marriage Encounter is a voluntary organization which offers residential and non-residential programmes for married and engaged couples to review and deepen their relationship by developing a compelling vision for their marriage and providing the communication skills to support this.

Peter and Janet Cox, 5 Hillside Way, Welwyn, Herts AL6 OTY
Tel. and Fax: 01438 715337;
email: *peter_janet_cox@hotmail.com*

Family Life and Marriage Education Network

A church network launched in 1990. Most dioceses are involved and there are often local officers. FLAME aims to co-ordinate, support and sustain the work of family life and marriage as a network for the exchange of information and expertise.

Tel. 01622 755014; Fax: 01622 693531;
email: *flame@csr.org.uk* http://www.welcome.to/familylife

The Mothers' Union

The Mothers' Union is an Anglican organization which promotes the well-being of families worldwide. This is done through developing prayer and spiritual growth in families, studying and reflecting on family life and its place in society and resourcing members to take practical action to improve conditions for families, both nationally and in the communities in which they live.

Mary Sumner House, 24 Tufton St., London SW1P 3RB

Tel. 020 7222 5533; Fax: 020 7222 1591;
email: *mu@themothersunion.org* Web: *www.themothersunion.org*

Relate (formerly National Marriage Guidance Council)
Offers counselling and psychosexual therapy to those who seek advice with adult couple relationships, whether married or not. *Relate* also publishes a wide range of helpful literature available from its bookshop. *Relate* local contacts can be found in the local telephone directory.

Herbert Gray College, Little Church St, Rugby, Warks CV21 3AP
Tel. 01788 573241; Fax: 01788 535007

Appendix 3
Comparison of the structures of Marriage Services

The Book of Common Prayer 1662	*Alternative Services, First Series (1966)*
Rubric on the publication of Banns	The Introduction
The Preface	Appeal for Impediments
Appeal for Impediments	THE MARRIAGE
The Espousals (questions of consent)	Questions of consent
Question (Who giveth this Woman to be married to this Man?)	Question (Who giveth this woman to be married to this man?)
The Vows	The Vows (option on 'obey')
Giving of the Ring	Blessing of the Ring
Prayer	Prayer
Declaration of the Marriage	Declaration of the Marriage
Blessing	Blessing
Psalm 128 or Psalm 67	THE BLESSING OF THE MARRIAGE
Kyrie Eleison	Psalm 128 or 67 or 37.3-7
Lord's Prayer	Kyrie Eleison
Versicles and Responses	Lord's Prayer
Prayers	Versicles and Responses
Exhortation	Prayers
(The phrase 'if there is no sermon' refers to the subsequent Communion, which it is convenient that the married couple should receive).	Blessing of the Couple
	Sermon and/or Reading from Scripture
	or
	Holy Communion

The Alternative Service Book 1980	Common Worship

The Introduction
Sentence 1: John 4.16
Greeting
Prayer
Readings and/or a Psalm may be
    used and/or a Hymn may
    be sung
A Sermon may be preached
	Pastoral Introduction
	Structure

The Marriage Service
Preface
Appeal for Impediment to the
    congregation
Appeal for impediment to the
    couple
Questions of Consent
Rubric on receiving the bride
The Vows (Option A or B)
Blessing of the Ring(s)
Exchange of the Ring(s)
Declaration of the Marriage
Blessing of the Couple
Acclamations
The Registration (now or at the
    end of the service)
Reading and Sermon (if not
    used earlier)
Psalm 67 or 121 or 128 or a Hymn
	Introduction
	The Welcome
	Preface
	The Declarations
	The Collect
	Readings
	Sermon
	
	The Marriage
	The Vows
	The Giving of the Rings
	The Proclamation
	The Blessing of the Marriage
	Registration of the Marriage
	    (optional position)
	Prayers
	The Dismissal

The Prayers The Lord's Prayer Blessing of the Couple and the Congregation	

Appendix 4
Resource list

The rather obvious problem with providing resources for a new service is that resources follow the publication of the service. There will be a wealth of new material to support the whole *Common Worship* process but here a general list of published resources is provided to enable ministers to keep up with changes as they occur.

Rosemary Gallagher, *Getting Married*, Chawton, Redemptorist Press, 1998 (ISBN 0 8523 1169 9).

Ewen Gilchrist, *A Church Wedding*, Oxford, Lion, 1999 (ISBN 0 7459 41273).

David Male, *The Marriage Service: A Guide*, London, Hodder & Stoughton, 1996 (ISBN 0 340 64199 1).

Marriage: A Teaching Document from the House of Bishops of the Church of England, London, Church House Publishing, 1999 (ISBN 0 7151 3829 4).

Marriage, London, Church House Publishing/The National Society, 1999. (An explanatory leaflet.)

An Order of Marriage for Christians from Different Churches, The Joint Liturgical Group of Great Britain, Canterbury Press Norwich (ISBN 1 85311 309 3).

Matrimony with Hymns, Alternative Services, First Series, London, SPCK, 1968 (ISBN 0 281 02377 8).

Michael Perry and Rowena Edlin-White, *Design your own Wedding Ceremony*, London, Marshall Pickering, 1997 (ISBN 0 551 03024 0).

Charles Read, *Revising Weddings* (Grove Worship 128), Nottingham, Grove Books Limited, 1994 (ISBN 1 08517 4263 8).

Stuart Thomas, *Your Wedding in the Church of England*, Bury St Edmunds, Kevin Mayhew, 1996 (ISBN 0 86209 802 5).

Mary Thompson, *Your Wedding* (A promotional leaflet available through Ecclesiastical Insurance).

Appendix 5
Copyright

It is essential that the Order of Service acknowledges the copyright owner (usually but not always the author) of hymns not in the public domain (generally for a period of seventy years after the author's death). It should also contain the church's CCLI licence reference. Remember also to make the necessary record of use. The address is: Christian Copyright Licensing International, P.O. Box 1339, Eastbourne BN21 4YF; Tel: 01323 417711; Fax: 01323 417722; email: copyright@ccli.co.uk   Web: *www.ccli.co.uk*

Reproduction of all or part of the text of *Common Worship*: Marriage is covered by the usual copyright conditions, as outlined in *A Brief Guide to Liturgical Copyright* (Church House Publishing, 2000, ISBN: 0 7151 8112 2, £1.50).

Further advice about all aspects of producing local orders of service is contained in Mark Earey, *Producing Your Own Orders of Service* (CHP/*Praxis*, 2000, ISBN: 0 7151 2001 8, £7.95).

Both titles are available from Church House Bookshop, 31 Great Smith Street, London, SW1P 3BN. Telephone: 020 7898 1301/2; Fax: 020 7898 1305; email: bookshop@c-of-e-org.uk   Web: *www.chbookshop.co.uk*

Appendix 6
The Faculty Office

This is the point of contact for any queries on marriage and the law and I have always found the staff to be most helpful and available. The Office publishes the booklet *Anglican Marriage in England and Wales: A Guide to the Law for Clergy* (Faculty Office of the Archbishop of Canterbury, 1992/1999) which is sent to all licensed clergy of the Church of England and the Church in Wales. Further copies are readily available at a cost of £3.50 each from the Registrar, Faculty Office, 1 The Sanctuary, Westminster, London, SW1P 3JT. Tel. 020 7222 5381 Ext. 2262; Fax: 020 7222 7502. (Office hours: 10 a.m. – 4 p.m. (Monday–Friday)).
Email: faculty.office@1Thesanctuary.com
Web: *www.facultyoffice.org.uk*

Index